D1274622

Saved by Grace

Saved by Grace

A Study of the Five Points of Calvinism

SECOND EDITION

by
Ronald Cammenga
& Ronald Hanko

Reformed Free Publishing Association
Grandville, Michigan

Printed in the United States of America

No part of this book may be used or reprinted in any form
without written permission from the publisher, except in the
case of brief quotations used in a critical article or review

The second edition is revised from the original edition,
which was copyrighted in 1995 by the Reformed Free
Publishing Association

Bible quotations are taken from the Authorized (King
James) Version unless otherwise noted

Book design by Jeff Steenholdt and Nighthawk Design

Reformed Free Publishing Association
4949 Ivanrest Ave., S.W.
Grandville, MI 49418-9709 USA
Phone: (616) 224-1518
Fax: (616) 224-1517
Website: www.rfpa.org
E-mail: mail@rfpa.org

ISBN 0-916206-74-2 (hardcover)
ISBN 0-916206-72-6 (paperback)
LC Control Number 2001119735

Dedicated to

the late Professor Homer C. Hoeksema, who in his teaching, preaching, and writing not only ably defended the Five Points of Calvinism, but also endeared them to students, church members, and readers alike.

Contents

Foreword

This is not your standard treatise on the "Five Points of Calvinism" or, as these grand truths are also called, "the doctrines of grace."

There is the clear, biblical explanation of the doctrines remembered by *"TULIP"* that one might find elsewhere.

But this work is a *consistent* exposition of God's sovereignty in the gracious salvation of sinners. It does not suffer from the confusion, contradiction, and compromise that characterize many similar efforts: God elected some but wills to save all; the natural man is totally depraved but performs many good works; Christ died only for the elect but "is dead" for everyone who hears the gospel; the actual saving of sinners is by irresistible grace but must take place by a "well-meant offer" made alike to all.

Saved by Grace is a *thorough* exposition of the truth of salvation by grace alone. It neither ignores nor softens the especially offensive aspects of the five points: the wickedness of *all* the deeds of the unregenerated, the eternal reprobation of some persons, the exclusion of some from the atonement of Christ and from all its benefits, the will of God with the preaching of the gospel that it harden some who hear.

Here is a *bold* defense of the gospel of grace. The book answers the objections. It exposes and destroys the foes (within the sphere of professing Calvinists as well as without the camp). It flies the banner of full, consistent Calvinism with never a trace of shame.

Saved by Grace

The reason in the end is simply the living knowledge of the triune God as revealed in Jesus Christ as really sovereign.

Such an exposition of the doctrines that make up the gospel is the need of our, and every other, time.

DAVID J. ENGELSMA, Professor
Protestant Reformed Seminary
Grandville, Michigan

Preface to the Second Edition

When the first edition of *Saved by Grace* was released, we could not have hoped that in a few short years our publisher would sell all the books that were printed, but to our surprise, this is what has happened. We are truly gratified at the response to its publication and for the necessity of a second edition.

Especially gratifying has been the extensive use to which the book has been put. Pastors have used it for the instruction of young people. Bible study societies have discussed it. Those new to the Reformed faith have been brought to a clearer understanding of the doctrines of grace. Long-time Calvinists have expressed their thanks that the book deepened their understanding and convictions.

The necessity of republishing has provided us with the opportunity to revise. The Table of Contents now gives subject subheadings. Although the main content of the book remains unchanged, there has been some reorganization, a few additions to the chapters, and minor editing of the text. Added to the back of the book are a table comparing Arminianism with Calvinism and an index for creedal citations. We hope that these changes will make *Saved by Grace* a continued resource for both teachers and students.

RONALD L. CAMMENGA
RONALD H. HANKO

Preface to the First Edition

This is a book about Calvinism. Specifically it is a book about what are known as the Five Points of Calvinism, commonly referred to as the doctrines of grace.

The reader must not make the mistake of identifying Calvinism with the "Five Points." Calvinism is more than merely five points of doctrine. Calvinism is a whole system, an orderly arrangement of all the cardinal truths of the Word of God. More than that, it is a world-and-life-view that concerns every area of earthly life: marriage and family, education and labor, church and society, entertainment and leisure, and much more. Nevertheless, the "Five Points" get at the heart of what Calvinism is.

Calvinism gets its name from the sixteenth century Protestant reformer John Calvin. More than any before him, Calvin developed and systematized these truths, especially in his well-known work *Institutes of the Christian Religion.* For this reason, although Calvinism by no means originated with Calvin, the system bears his name.

Historically the most eminent defense of Calvinism was carried on by the famed Synod of Dordrecht, 1618–1619. This synod, with representatives from Reformed churches all over the world, condemned the teaching of the Arminians, or Remonstrants, and reaffirmed the precious truths of Calvinism. Since the Arminians had expressed their doctrinal position in five key statements, the decisions of the synod were organized in a fivefold way. Thus the "Five Points" of Calvinism.

There remains today much antagonism toward Calvinism. Many even in Reformed and Presbyterian churches are ignorant of the Five Points of Calvinism, their own ecclesiastical heritage. In our spiritually illiterate age, misunderstanding and misconceptions also abound.

This book is an effort to correct this sad situation. We have attempted to set forth the Five Points of Calvinism in a straight-forward, easy-to-understand way. The book is written with the "ordinary" Christian in mind. With a view to convincing the unconvinced, the book is saturated with proof texts. We have made every effort to let the Scriptures (and God through them) speak. We also trust that the book will foster a deeper appreciation for the truths of Calvinism among those who do already consider themselves Calvinists.

This is our first attempt at book writing. We beg the indulgence of our readers. Our prayer is that the Lord will bless our feeble efforts for the cause of the advancement of His truth, for "except the Lord build the house, they labor in vain that build it" (Ps. 127:1).

Ronald L. Cammenga
Ronald H. Hanko

CHAPTER I

The Sovereignty of God

One scriptural truth distinguishes what is known as the Reformed faith, or Calvinism. That truth is the sovereignty of God.

Many people suppose that the heart of Calvinism is its teaching of predestination. When they hear of Calvinism or that someone is a Calvinist, they may immediately think of election and reprobation.

It is true that the doctrine of predestination has an important place in the teaching of Calvinism, as it did in the teaching of John Calvin himself. Nevertheless, predestination is not the central truth of the Reformed faith. The heart of Calvinism is not the doctrine of predestination or, for that matter, any one of the other Five Points of Calvinism. The central truth proclaimed by Calvinism—Calvinism that is faithful to its heritage—is the *absolute sovereignty of God*. Calvin saw the essential place that the confession of the sovereignty of God has in relation to the whole body of biblical truth: "Unless we fully believe this [God's sovereignty] the very beginning of our faith is periled, by which we profess to believe in God ALMIGHTY."[1]

The distinguishing feature of the Reformed faith is unquestionably its conception of God. *What we believe about God matters most.* Everything else that we believe stands connected to and is affected by what we believe about God. The most important question that any man faces is, "Who is

God?" It is true, as Calvin writes in the opening paragraph of his *Institutes of the Christian Religion,* that all ". . . true and sound wisdom, consists of two parts: the knowledge of God and of ourselves."[2] But as he goes on to say, "It is certain that man never achieves a clear knowledge of himself unless he has first looked upon God's face, and then descends from contemplating him to scrutinize himself."[3] This knowledge of God is not merely of great importance; it is the chief end of man. The opening question of the Westminster Shorter Catechism asks, "What is the chief end of man?" The answer is, "Man's chief end is to glorify God, and to enjoy him forever." But man cannot glorify God or enjoy Him if man does not *know* God. Man's chief end and calling, therefore, is to know God.

Not only is the knowledge of God man's highest calling, it is also his greatest good. Jesus teaches that in John 17:3: "And this is life eternal, that they might know thee the only true God, and Jesus Christ, whom thou hast sent." Salvation itself consists in knowing God. Those who have eternal life possess a *right* and *saving knowledge* of God.

Knowledge of God begins with the affirmation of faith that God is and that God is sovereign. Since God is, He must be sovereign. If God is not sovereign, the inescapable implication is that He is not God.

The sovereignty of God is the great issue that divides true religion and false religion. This is the great issue that separates the true church of Jesus Christ in the world from the false and apostate church. This is the issue that distinguishes faith from unbelief.

The confession of God's sovereignty is gladly and thankfully made by every believer. It is the teaching about God set forth in the infallible Scriptures, the source of our knowledge about God. And this is the truth confessed about God by Reformed (or Calvinistic) Christians.

A. The doctrine

God's sovereignty is His absolute authority and rule over all things. To say that God is sovereign is to say that God is God. Because He is God, He does as He pleases, only as He pleases, and always as He pleases. That God is sovereign means that He is the Lord, the Ruler, the Master, the King. The one who confesses the sovereignty of God confesses that God is almighty, omnipotent, and the only one who exercises all power in heaven and on earth. To confess the sovereignty of God is to confess that nothing is outside of God's control, but that all things take place according to His will and appointment.

Two fundamental truths stand at the basis of God's sovereignty. The first is the oneness of God. God is God alone. There is no other god than the Lord God. Obviously, two cannot be almighty. Two cannot be omnipotent. Two cannot be sovereign. God is sovereign because He, and He alone, is God.

Second, the sovereignty of God rests on the truth that He is the Creator. God has made everything that exists. By His almighty power He brought everything into existence in the beginning, calling "those things which be not as though they were" (Rom. 4:17). The entire universe owes its existence to God. By virtue of the fact that He is the Creator, God is sovereign over all things.

Parents have the right to rule over their children. God gives them that right because the children are their children. In God's providence the parents have conceived them and have brought them forth into the world, thereby giving them their life and existence. If this is true of earthly parents in relationship to their children, how much more is this not true of God in relationship to the universe!

God's sovereignty is an *absolute* sovereignty. By this we mean that God's sovereignty is over everything and everyone. *Nothing* is excluded from God's sovereign control. God rules in the realm of the natural, exercising His power over inanimate creatures as well as the brute creation. God rules over men and angels, time and history, the world and the church. God's rule extends not only to those circumstances we regard as good, but also to the bad: sickness, famine, tornadoes, floods, hurricanes, and earthquakes. Beyond this, God is sovereign even over sin and sinners, the devil and the demons of hell. They do nothing apart from His sovereign will.

Not only is God absolutely sovereign in the realm of the natural, but He must be and is sovereign also in salvation. God's sovereignty in salvation means that God saves whom He wills to save, and there is no power able to frustrate the sovereign power of God at work in the saving of the sinner: not the natural obstinacy of the sinner himself, not the power of the devil (formidable though it is), not the opposition of the wicked world (intense though it may be), are able to stand in the way of the sovereignty of God. None of those can frustrate the sovereign power of God in salvation, but under His sovereignty they actually serve the ultimate salvation of God's people.

B. Scripture proofs
    1. God's sovereignty affirmed
        a. Job 42:2: "I know that thou canst do every thing, and that no thought can be withholden from thee."

Job acknowledges that God can do everything—in other words, that God is sovereign. He goes on to state the implications of this, namely, that no one can "withhold" or prevent from being realized any thought in the mind of God. What God wills and plans He is always able to bring to pass.

        b. Psalm 115:3: "But our God is in the heavens: *he hath done whatsoever he hath pleased.*"

God's sovereignty is affirmed by the statement of the psalmist that God is "in the heavens." He is not an earthly creature, finite and limited. This affirmation is strengthened when he adds, "he hath done whatsoever he hath pleased." What God pleases, that is, what He wills, He does. With us men it is different. It is very well possible that we determine something but are unable to do it. We deal with this frustration daily. I want to drive somewhere, but if my car has broken down, I am prevented from carrying out what I wish, or will, to do. What God wills, He is able to accomplish. *Nothing* is able to frustrate His will, because He is sovereign.

> c. Isaiah 14:24, 27: "The LORD of hosts hath sworn, saying, *Surely as I have thought, so shall it come to pass; and as I have purposed, so shall it stand* . . . For the LORD of hosts hath purposed, and who shall disannul it? and his hand is stretched out, and who shall turn it back?"

What God thinks comes to pass; what He purposes stands. Nothing is able to contravene God's sovereignty. When Isaiah asks, "Who shall disannul it?" the obvious answer is, "No one!" And when he asks, "Who shall turn it back?" the implied answer is again, "No one!"

> d. Isaiah 46:9, 10: "Remember the former things of old: for I am God, and there is none else; I am God, and there is none like me, Declaring the end from the beginning, and from ancient times the things that are not yet done, saying, My counsel shall stand, and *I will do all my pleasure.*"

God's counsel stands, that is, comes to pass just as He has willed it. God does all His good pleasure, everything He pleases. This happens because "There is none else; . . . there is none like me."

> e. Daniel 4:34, 35: "And at the end of the days I Nebuchadnezzar lifted up mine eyes unto heaven, and mine understanding returned unto me, and I blessed the most High, and I praised and honoured him that liveth for ever, whose dominion is an everlasting dominion, and his kingdom is from generation to generation: And all the inhabitants of the earth are reputed as nothing: and *he doeth according to his will in the army of heaven, and among the inhabitants of the earth: and none can stay his hand,* or say unto him, What doest thou?"

In His sovereignty God does as He wills in the army of heaven and among the inhabitants of the earth. Heaven and earth—all things—are included in His sovereign control. What makes this such a striking confession of the sovereignty of God is that it is a confession made by an unbelieving man—King Nebuchadnezzar. Even such a wicked man is forced not only to see, but also to acknowledge, God's sovereignty.

Nebuchadnezzar had experienced that sovereignty of God in his own life, for God had taken Nebuchadnezzar's kingdom away from him and humbled that proud king by making him as a beast of the field. Nebuchadnezzar had gloried in his own power and fancied himself the master of his own destiny: "Is not this great Babylon, that I have built for the house of the kingdom by the might of my power, and for the honor of my majesty?" (Dan. 4:30). He had denied and defied God's sovereignty. Then God had demonstrated His sovereignty to Nebuchadnezzar, demonstrating it to him in such a way that he would not soon forget. Those who deny God's sovereign prerogatives are subject to similar lessons!

    f.   Ephesians 1:11: "In whom also we have obtained an inheritance, being predestinated according to the purpose of him who worketh *all things* after the counsel of his own will."

This text is speaking about Jesus Christ, the Son of God. As the Son of God, He works all things according to His will.

    g.   1 Timothy 6:15: "Which in his times he shall shew, who is the blessed and only Potentate, the King of kings, and Lord of lords."

God is the King of kings and the Lord of lords. He is exalted over the rulers of this world. And if God rules over the highest earthly dignitaries, He rules over everything in this world.

    h.   Revelation 11:16, 17: "And the four and twenty elders, which sat before God on their seats, fell upon their faces, and worshipped God, Saying, We give thee thanks, O Lord God Almighty, which art, and wast, and art to come; because thou hast taken to thee thy great power, and hast reigned."

In this passage God's sovereignty is taught in two ways. First, He is called "Lord God Almighty." That God is Lord and that He is Almighty indicate His sovereignty. Second, it is said about Him that He has taken to himself "great power, and hast reigned." That God takes to Himself "great" power— the greatest power—and that He reigns—reigns alone, and reigns notwithstanding the defiance of His enemies—means that He is sovereign.

---

  i. Isaiah 42:8: "I am the LORD: that is my name: and my glory will I not give to another, neither my praise to graven images."

 2. God's sovereignty over the brute creation
  a. Genesis 1, 2: the creation account

Because God is absolutely sovereign, He is sovereign over the brute creation. When God said, "Let there be light," there was light. When God said, "Let there be a firmament," the firmament appeared. When God called forth the animals, they did not begin a long evolutionary development of several million years, but they came forth into existence. And so it was with the entire creation.

  b. Miracles like the flood (Gen. 7), the ten plagues sent by God on Egypt (Ex. 8–12), Israel's crossing of the Red Sea (Ex. 14), the sending of the manna (Ex. 16), the standing still of the sun (Josh. 10), the calming of the storm (Luke 8), the feeding of the 4,000 (Matt. 15), and countless others all point to God's sovereignty over the creation and every creature in the creation. This is why it is necessary for the church today to defend the miracles that are recorded in the Holy Scriptures. To deny the miracles is not only to deny the infallibility of the Bible but also the sovereignty of God. Because the Christian believes the sovereignty of God, he has no difficulty accepting the miracles taught in the Bible. Because he believes the sovereignty of God, the Christian looks forward eagerly to the miracles prophesied in the Bible: the second coming of Jesus Christ, the resurrection of our dead bodies, and the creation of a new heavens and a new earth in which righteousness shall dwell.

c. Psalm 103:19: "The LORD hath prepared his throne in the heavens; and *his kingdom ruleth over all.*"

Since God's throne (the symbol of power) is in the heavens (above the earth), and His kingdom rules over all, the entire creation is subject to His sovereign control.

d. Psalm 135:6, 7: "Whatsoever the LORD pleased, that did he in heaven, and in earth, in the seas, and all deep places. He causeth the vapours to ascend from the ends of the earth; he maketh the lightnings for the rain; he bringeth the wind out of his treasuries."

God's sovereignty, according to this passage, extends to heaven, the earth, the seas, and all deep places. Dew, lightning, rain, and wind are under the controlling hand of God. "It" does not rain; God causes rain. "It" does not blow; God sends the wind. That it rains, where it rains, how much it rains—all are determined by God.

e. Matthew 10:29, 30: "Are not two sparrows sold for a farthing? and one of them shall not fall on the ground without your Father. But the very hairs of your head are all numbered."

The sovereign rule of God extends to what we would call "insignificant" sparrows, and even to (who would think of it!) the hairs of our heads. If sparrows and hair are under the sovereignty of God, it is safe to conclude that everything is under His sovereign rule.

3. God's sovereignty over men and the affairs of men's lives
   a. Proverbs 16:9: "A man's heart deviseth his way: but the LORD directeth his steps."

Man may set goals and make plans, but God "directeth" the course of man's life. What a man does, where he goes, what he accomplishes, are determined by the sovereign God.

   b. Proverbs 16:33: "The lot is cast into the lap; but the whole disposing thereof is of the Lord."

In Bible times issues were often decided, or people chosen, by means of the casting of lots. For example, when the children of Israel came into the land of Canaan, each tribe received its specific portion of the land of Canaan by the casting of lots: "Notwithstanding the land shall be divided by lot: according to the names of the tribes of their fathers they shall inherit. According to the lot shall the possession thereof be divided between many and few" (Num. 26:55, 56). The outcome of the casting of lots might appear to be random, purely arbitrary, but Solomon says in Proverbs 16:33 that that is not the case. The "disposing," that is, the result of the casting of lots, is under the control of God. Clearly, God rules over men and the activity of men.

   c. Proverbs 21:1: "The king's heart is in the hand of the LORD, as the rivers of water: he turneth it whithersoever he will."

Not just the king's actions, but the very heart of the king is in the hand of God. In the Scriptures the heart is the center and seat of man's entire life. If God controls the king's heart, He controls the king. And if God controls the king, the greatest of men, He controls all those who are under the king. In other words, all men, high and low, great and small, mighty and insignificant, are subject to the sovereign will of an almighty God.

    d. Jeremiah 10:23: "O LORD, I know that the way of man is not in himself: it is not in man that walketh to direct his steps."

Man, Jeremiah says, does not direct the course of his own footsteps. His way in life is not "in himself." He lives an active life in the world, but ultimately it is God who directs the course of every man's life.

    4. God's sovereignty over the evils and adversities of earthly life

There is a popular misconception today that only good comes from the hand of God and is therefore under His control. The bad things, life's troubles and earthly distresses, it is supposed, are the work of the devil. Thus, health and prosperity come from God, while the sudden death of a young mother or the disaster caused by an earthquake are from the devil. The Bible teaches us quite differently.

    a. Genesis 50:20: "But as for you, ye thought evil against me; but God meant it unto good, to bring to pass, as it is this day, to save much people alive."

Great calamity had befallen Joseph. He had been thrown into a pit, sold as a slave, and carried to Egypt, separated from family and friends and even imprisoned for a time. In his afflictions Joseph never lost sight of the truth of the sovereignty of God. God, he says, was the one who brought all those calamities to pass. And God did it for good. Not only did Joseph confess God's sovereignty, but it is plain that he enjoyed its comfort.

> b. Job 1:21: "And [Job] said, Naked came I out of my mother's womb, and naked shall I return thither: *the LORD gave, and the LORD hath taken away;* blessed be the name of the LORD."
>
> c. Job 2:10: "But he [Job] said unto her, Thou speakest as one of the foolish women speaketh. What? shall we receive good at the hand of God, and shall we not receive evil? In all this did not Job sin with his lips."

Job spoke these words at a time in his life when he was enduring extreme suffering. He had lost all his earthly possessions, his cattle, his servants, and even his ten children. Satan and Job's enemies had been the instruments to bring these afflictions into his life. But Job understood the truth of the sovereignty of God. Behind Satan and the wicked Sabeans and Chaldeans, Job saw the mighty hand of God. He does not say, "The LORD gave, and the devil and my enemies have now taken it all away." Oh no! "The LORD gave, and *the LORD* hath taken away." Not only had Job received good at the hand of God (riches, cattle, servants, and children), but he had also received evil (the loss of all these things) from the hand of God.

> 5. God's sovereignty over sin and the sinner
>> a. Genesis 45:7, 8: "And God sent me before you to preserve you a posterity in the earth, and to save your lives by a great deliverance. So now it was not you that sent me hither, but God: and he hath made me a father to Pharaoh, and lord of all his house, and a ruler throughout all the land of Egypt."

Joseph was sold into slavery into Egypt by the sinfulness of his brothers, yet he was able to see the sovereignty of God ruling even over the sinful deed of his brothers. Very really it was the brothers who had sent Joseph down into Egypt. But Joseph, because he understood the truth of God's sovereignty, teaches that it was God who had sent him down to Egypt.

> b. 2 Samuel 16:10: "And the king [David] said, What have I to do with you, ye sons of Zeruiah? so let him [Shimei] curse, because the LORD hath said unto him, Curse David. Who shall then say, Wherefore hast thou done so?"

At the time David spoke these words, he was fleeing from his own son Absalom, who had usurped David's throne. Added to his suffering of having to flee for his life from his own son, he was also made to suffer the reproach and blasphemy of wicked Shimei. Two of David's captains, the brothers Joab and Abishai, wanted to kill Shimei for his wicked reproach to David. But David forbade them because "The LORD hath said unto him, Curse David." Behind the sinful deed of Shimei, David saw the sovereign hand of God. David was content that the sovereign God would avenge the sin of Shimei in His own time and in His own way.

> c. Isaiah 45:7: "I form the light, and create darkness: *I* make peace, and *create evil:* I the LORD do all these things."

In this passage the Lord Himself is speaking. He affirms His sovereignty over evil: "I . . . create evil." If the Lord creates evil, certainly He is sovereign over the evil.

> d. Amos 3:6: "Shall a trumpet be blown in the city,

and the people not be afraid? Shall there be evil in
a city, and the LORD hath not done it?"

As certainly as the blowing of the warning trumpet made the
inhabitants of a city afraid of the attack by the enemy, so certainly when there is evil in a city, that evil is brought by the
Lord. In this way we are taught that the Lord *appoints*, brings,
and controls evil.

    e. Luke 22:22: "And truly the Son of man goeth, as it
       was determined: but woe unto that man by whom
       he is betrayed."
    f. Acts 2:23: "Him [Christ] being delivered by the de-
       terminate counsel and foreknowledge of God, ye
       have taken, and by wicked hands have crucified
       and slain."

Both of these texts teach the sovereignty of God over the very
worst sin ever committed—the crucifying of Jesus Christ.
Wicked men crucified Him and were to blame, to be sure, for
their sinful deed. But even Christ's crucifixion took place according to the sovereign appointment and under the almighty
control of God. If God was sovereign over the worst sin, certainly He is sovereign over all sin.

    6. God's sovereignty in salvation
      a. Matthew 11:25, 26: "At that time Jesus answered
        and said, I thank thee, O Father, Lord of heaven and
        earth, because thou hast hid these things from the
        wise and prudent, and hast revealed them unto babes.
        Even so, Father: for so it seemed good in thy sight."

By these words Jesus clearly teaches the sovereignty of God in
salvation. God hides the things of the kingdom of heaven from

certain men with the result that they are not saved. God reveals the things of the kingdom to other men with the result that they are saved. Both the hiding and the revealing take place according to the sovereign will of God: "for so it seemed good in thy sight."

> b. Acts 16:14: "And a certain woman named Lydia, a seller of purple, of the city of Thyatira, which worshipped God, heard us: whose heart the Lord opened, that she attended unto the things which were spoken of Paul."

Lydia was saved. Although she was saved by means of the preaching of the apostle Paul, it was not Paul who saved her. Lydia believed Paul's preaching, but she did not save herself by the power of her own free will. Lydia's salvation was due to this: *the* LORD opened her heart, as He does the heart of every sinner who is saved.

> c. Romans 9:18: "Therefore hath he mercy on whom he will have mercy, and whom he will he hardeneth."

The apostle Paul teaches that God shows mercy to those men and women to whom He wills to show mercy. Since God's mercy is the cause of our salvation, we may understand Paul to be teaching that God saves whom He wills to save. Not only that, but those who are *not* saved, are not saved because God hardens them in their sin and unbelief: "and whom he will he hardeneth."

God's sovereignty in salvation is also clearly taught in a multitude of Scripture passages that speak of God efficaciously saving sinners. God does not just try to save sinners, all the while depending on their willingness to be saved. He does not attempt to save them and then stand by helplessly when they do not cooperate with Him by using their free will to be saved. He does not do His best to save sinners, always facing the real possibility that His best is not good enough and that the sinner may effectively resist His efforts to save him. No, God does not offer salvation to sinners. He saves sinners—sovereignly, efficaciously, and irresistibly! This is always how the Scriptures describe salvation.

d. Matthew 1:21: "And she shall bring forth a son, and thou shalt call his name JESUS: for he *shall* save his people from their sins."

e. 1 Corinthians 1:21: "For after that in the wisdom of God the world by wisdom knew not God, it pleased God by the foolishness of preaching to save them that believe."

f. Ephesians 2:4, 5: "But God, who is rich in mercy, for his great love wherewith he loved us, Even when we were dead in sins, hath quickened us together with Christ, (by grace ye *are saved*)."

g. 2 Timothy 1:9: "Who *hath saved* us, and called us with an holy calling, not according to our works, but according to his own purpose and grace, which was given us in Christ Jesus before the world began."

h. 2 Timothy 1:12: "For the which cause I also suffer these things: nevertheless I am not ashamed: for I know whom I have believed, and am persuaded that he is able to keep that which I have committed unto him against that day."

What Paul has committed to God is his soul's salvation, which He is confident that God is able to keep. What explains the confidence of Paul? How can he be sure that he will be kept in salvation notwithstanding the devil, the wicked world, and his own sinful flesh? He can have that confidence only because of his belief in God's sovereignty. Because God sovereignly brought him to salvation, he can be sure that God will also sovereignly preserve him in salvation.

C. Objections

Historically two objections have been lodged against the biblical, Reformed teaching of the sovereignty of God. First, it has been charged that the teaching of God's sovereignty makes God the author of sin. Second, it has been charged that to teach God's sovereignty is to deny man's responsibility.

1. "If God is sovereign, He is the author of sin."

This is the contention of the enemies of the Reformed faith. The argument is that if God has willed and by His almighty power brings about the evil, then God is to blame for the evil in the world. Since God is perfect, completely without any sin, and since evil does exist, God therefore cannot be sovereign.

There are some who have attempted to reconcile this seeming contradiction by teaching that God in His sovereignty only "permits" sin. Although He actively wills the good, He only passively allows the evil to take place. This is an unsatisfactory explanation. For one thing it does not resolve the problem. If I permit someone to be run over by a truck when I could have warned that person or prevented him from being run over, I am as responsible for his injury as if I had deliberately run over him myself. The point is that if God permits sin when He could prevent it, the same charge can be brought that God is responsible for sin.

Besides not solving the difficulty, to speak of God only permitting sin and evil does not do justice to the teaching of the Scriptures with regard to the sovereignty of God. God did not simply permit the devil to afflict Job, but through Job says, "The Lord gave, and the Lord hath taken away." God did not simply permit the crucifixion of Jesus Christ; Christ's crucifixion took place according to the "determinate counsel and foreknowledge of God" (Acts 2:23).

Our answer to the first objection is that the Scriptures are true—God is sovereign, sovereign even over sin and evil, but in such a way that He is not the author of, nor can He be charged with, the sins that wicked men commit (Ezek. 18:25–30; Acts 2:23, 24; Rom. 9:10–18). Although God is sovereign over sin, the sinner sins willingly, desires to sin, delights in sin, and actively commits the sin. The sinner is not compelled against his will to sin. He is not forced to sin although he does not want to sin. God effects the evil in such a way that Satan and wicked men willingly perform it. As James says in James 1:13, 14, "Let no man say when he is tempted, I am tempted of God: for God cannot be tempted with evil, neither tempteth he any man: But every man is tempted, when he is drawn away of his own lust, and enticed."

That God cannot be charged with being the author of sin is further evident from *His purpose in decreeing sin.* Unlike Satan and wicked men, God's purpose with sin is a good purpose. His purpose is His own glory through the demonstration of the glorious perfections of His Being. His purpose is the demonstration of His power that is able to make even sin and the sinner subservient to His will. His purpose is the demonstration of His righteousness, which demands and accomplishes satisfaction for sin. His purpose is the demonstration of His free grace that saves not "good people" but unworthy sinners in the cross of Christ. God's purpose in decreeing sin is the revelation of Himself in His Son Jesus Christ, the Savior from sin.

2. "If God is sovereign, man is not responsible for his sin."

This is the second objection that is often made against the teaching of the sovereignty of God. The argument is that if God sovereignly wills and brings about sin and evil, what else can a man do *but* sin? Hence, man cannot be held accountable for the evil that he does.

The apostle Paul deals with this objection to divine sovereignty in Romans 9. The objection is brought in verse 19: "Thou wilt say then unto me, Why doth he [God] yet find fault? For who hath resisted his will?" What is Paul's answer to this objection? Does he concede the objection? Not at all. Listen: "Nay but, O man, who art thou that repliest against God? Shall the thing formed say to him that formed it, Why hast thou made me thus?" (v. 20).

God is sovereign, even over sin and the sinner, but God is sovereign over sin and the sinner in such a way that the sinner himself always remains responsible before God for his sin. Yes, the Son of Man goes to the cross as it was determined by God: "But woe unto that man by whom he is betrayed" (Luke 22:22). To be sure, Christ is delivered by the determinate counsel and foreknowledge of God, but it is also true that "wicked hands" are responsible for His being crucified and slain (Acts 2:23).

Nor is this truth ever a real problem for the sinner. In our everyday life we experience no tension between God's sovereignty and our own responsibility. Although we believe that all things are under the sovereign control of God, we know that when we do wrong, we are responsible for the wrong we have done. We feel the guilt and must also face the consequences. In a way that surpasses our ability to comprehend it, *God is absolutely sovereign* and *man is responsible for his sin.*

D. Denials of God's sovereignty

The denial of the truth of the sovereignty of God takes many forms. There are theological denials and more practical denials.

1. Communist totalitarianism, fascism, and socialism

According to communist theory, and that of its first cousins, fascism and socialism, the state and the idea of the state is sovereign. The state owns everything. The state controls every area of life. The interests of the state are the only interests that are of any importance. This is a fundamental attack on the sovereignty of God. It is giving to the state those things that belong only to God. Given this teaching of communism, it is not surprising that the communist states have shown themselves hostile to Christianity. Communism is, in fact, inherently anti-God and anti-Christian.

2. Evolutionism

The teaching of evolution is that the world came into existence by mere chance. The continued existence of the world is due to the outworking of fixed natural laws and blind fate. Not only is evolution a rejection of the biblical creation account (Gen. 1–3), but evolution is also a fundamental denial of the sovereignty of God. It denies His sovereign power in creating the heavens and earth. It also denies the sovereignty of God in the upholding of the universe and the directing of the course of the world's history. There can be no compromise between the Reformed faith and evolution. The god of evolution (man) is not the sovereign God of the Bible. Those who today are attempting to compromise these two are guilty of attacking the very heart of the biblical Reformed faith—the sovereignty of God. If concessions are made to the theory of evolution, the truth of God's sovereignty is bartered away for a mess of humanistic pottage.

3. Pelagianism, Semi-Pelagianism, Arminianism, the free offer of the gospel, and free will

All of these false teachings, which will be discussed in more detail in the following chapters, have in common a denial of the sovereignty of God, particularly His sovereignty in the salvation of lost sinners. According to all these views, although God sincerely desires the salvation of all men, He is unable actually to accomplish the salvation of anyone. Although God wants to save a man, that man is in himself powerful enough to resist God's saving grace and frustrate God's intention to save him. Even after God has begun to save a man, regenerated him, given him His Holy Spirit and the gift of faith, it is possible for the man to fall away from grace and salvation— a falling away that God is unable to prevent. This is a blatant denial of God's sovereignty in salvation. It is no surprise that where these untruths have been accepted, the affirmation of the absolute sovereignty of God is no longer heard.

4. Humanism

The Renaissance—the revival of learning and the rediscovery of the ancient Greek and Roman writers that began in the fourteenth century and continued through the sixteenth century—gave birth to humanism. Renaissance thinkers promoted a confidence in human nature, a trust in man's native abilities, and an optimistic view of man's potential. It was this view of man that became known as humanism.

In the thinking of the humanist, man is the center of all things. Man is the master of his own destiny. Man's will is decisive and determinative. Man's mind is the final arbiter of truth. And man himself is the judge of what is right and what is wrong.

Religious humanism developed out of the secular humanism of the Renaissance. Men like Erasmus, Socinius, and Arminius promoted in the church what was basically a humanistic view of man. In our times much of evangelical Christianity has adopted many of the major tenets of humanism.

But humanism is a direct assault on the sovereignty of God. Humanism is nothing more than the original lie of the devil: "Ye shall be as gods" (Gen. 3:5). Humanism is the rejection of the absolute sovereignty of God and the exaltation of man to the throne of the universe. It will be the philosophy of humanism that will drive the engine of the coming antichristian kingdom. The number of Antichrist, according to Revelation 13:18, will be the number of man. But exactly because God alone is sovereign, the kingdom of Antichrist will not last, but is doomed to destruction. For that reason, "He that sitteth in the heavens shall laugh: the Lord shall have them in derision" (Ps. 2:4).

5. Deism

This teaching, more philosophy than religion, arose about the time of the American Revolution, especially in France. Deism taught that although God exists and that He created the world, at present He has no relation to the world. In other words, deism denies that God is everywhere present in the creation and that He is the God of providence, upholding and ruling all things in creation by His almighty power. Against the truth of God's sovereignty, the deists teach that though God may be sovereign, His sovereignty has no significance in time and history and therefore no significance for man's life.

Rather, all things develop according to natural laws, and it is up to man to determine his own destiny.

This denial of God's sovereignty needs to be mentioned, because it was the "religion" of many of the men who were leaders of the American Revolution and who wrote the Declaration of Independence and the American Constitution, men like Thomas Jefferson, Benjamin Franklin, and James Madison. So it is that the American Constitution and other documents connected with the history of the United States of America are founded on deist principles rather than on the biblical teaching of God's sovereignty.

This is especially clear from the second paragraph of the Declaration of Independence: "We hold these truths to be self-evident: that all men are created equal; that they are endowed by their Creator with certain unalienable rights; that among these are life, liberty, and the pursuit of happiness. That to secure these rights governments are instituted among men, deriving their just powers *from the consent of the governed.*"

A denial of God's sovereignty also lies at the base of the proud statement with which the Preamble to the American Constitution begins: "We the people . . ."

Apart from the fact that it is neither true nor biblical that all men are created equal and have certain unalienable rights (Deut. 7:6; Dan. 2:21; Luke 1:52; 1 Cor. 1:26), it is a blatant denial of God's sovereignty to teach that government derives its power from the consent of the governed and not from God (Rom. 13:1–7). And, as the Declaration goes on to say, "It is the right of the people to alter and abolish it [government], and to institute new government" as they see fit (paragraph 13).

The idea so common today that the American Constitution and Declaration of Independence are "Christian" documents is utterly false, and the simple fact that God is mentioned in them should not mislead people.

Along these same lines, we must condemn every form of rebellion and resistance against God-instituted government as a denial of the sovereign power and right of God as outlined in the first part of Romans 13.

6. Feminism

The heresy of feminism, which has swept through both human society and the church, is also a denial of God's sovereignty. It denies not just the headship of the man over the woman, but the headship of God, which is reflected in the man's headship over the woman and which is the foundation for his headship. Nor is it surprising that feminism has gained such a foothold in the visible church when the church, for the most part, no longer believes in the sovereignty of God.

That feminism is a denial of God's headship and thus also of His sovereignty is clear from those passages which show that the woman, in submitting to the headship of the man, submits also to God in Christ (1 Cor. 11:3; Eph. 5:22, 24; Col. 3:18).

7. The practice of believers

Even believers, from a practical point of view, are tempted to deny the sovereignty of God. It is one thing to confess this truth intellectually and abstractly; it is quite another to acknowledge this truth when the sovereignty of God touches our own lives personally. It is one thing to confess that God sovereignly rules over all so that nothing takes place by chance but according to His appointment; it is another to confess God's sovereignty when our crops have been devastated, our home destroyed, or we have lost our job. It is one thing to confess that the evils of this life are included in the sovereignty of God; it is another to confess the sovereignty of God at the graveside of a loved one. It is one thing to confess the sovereignty of God in salvation; it is quite another to confess the sovereignty of God when we see His sovereignty in election and reprobation being worked out in our own congregation, our own families, and even among our own children.

It takes the grace of God to confess and to submit to the sovereignty of God. It takes grace to confess that all things, and our own lives too, are under His control and subject to His will. It takes grace to confess, "The LORD gave, and the LORD hath taken away; blessed be the name of the LORD." Apart from sovereign grace, no man will ever confess the sovereignty of God. That a man does confess this is itself due to God's sovereignty.

E. Practical importance

The practical importance of the truth of the sovereignty of God cannot be overemphasized.

1. God's sovereignty and worship

Belief in God's sovereignty underlies the true worship of God. In the very first commandment of God's law we are confronted with the truth of God's sovereignty. Since God is God alone, He ought to be worshiped by us. Since God alone is sovereign, He alone ought to be worshiped. If our worship is to be proper worship—worship that exalts His greatness and acknowledges our unworthiness and inability—at the heart of it must be the confession of the sovereignty of God.

God's sovereignty not only demands that God be worshiped, but it determines as well the way in which we are to worship Him. If God is sovereign, He must not and cannot be represented by dumb images that cannot think, speak, or perform one action. If God is sovereign, our worship of Him must not be in ways of our choosing, but in harmony with His will. If God is sovereign, the almighty "I AM that I AM," our worship of Him must be reverent. The lack of reverence in so much of what passes for "Christian" worship today is symptomatic of the loss in the churches of the doctrine (truth) of God's sovereignty.

2. God's sovereignty and the glory of God

Certainly the importance of the truth of God's sovereignty is that it glorifies God. If the almighty power of God stands behind all that takes place in the world and is the cause of salvation besides, God is to be glorified. None of the glory belongs to man or to any other creature. Glory to God alone! This is man's great calling. Why has he been put on this earth? Why has God saved him? Why has God given him all that he has? So that he will glorify God. And God fully deserves that glory because He is sovereign, the almighty "I AM that I AM."

3. God's sovereignty and history

An understanding of the truth of God's sovereignty is necessary for a proper view of history, and so it is of great importance for Christian education. History is only properly understood and properly taught when it is viewed as the outworking of the sovereign counsel of God. God is in control, and God is executing His will. God sets up kings and casts them down from their thrones. God brings nations to power and causes their overthrow. God raised up Pharaoh, used him for His own purpose, and when He was finished, drowned him in the Red Sea. Similarly God brought Hitler to power, was sovereign over the bloodshed and devastation he perpetrated, and in the end, after Hitler had served God's purpose,

He brought his Third Reich to ruin. In the truest sense of the word, history is *His story.*

4. God's sovereignty and assurance

The truth of God's sovereignty is the foundation of the comfort of the people of God. Only if we know that God is in control—our God who is our Father for Jesus' sake—can we have the assurance that all is well. If there is some other power in this world besides the almighty power of our God, some power over which God does not have control, we must live in fear. But there is no such other power. God is *absolutely* sovereign, even over sin and evil, the devil and wicked men. That gives us the assurance that "*all* things work together for [our] good" (Rom. 8:28). Then we may be "persuaded, that neither death, nor life, nor angels, nor principalities, nor powers, nor things present, nor things to come, Nor height, nor depth, nor any other creature, shall be able to separate us from the love of God, which is in Christ Jesus our Lord" (Rom. 8:38, 39).

5. God's sovereignty and our preservation

Belief in the sovereignty of God is necessary for the assurance of each Christian's preservation in salvation and for the assurance of the final salvation of the church as a whole. If God is not sovereign, we must always be in doubt concerning our personal salvation, as well as the salvation of the entire church. In fact, if God is not sovereign, the salvation of even one child of God is impossible, because we were born hating God, totally depraved, and under the bondage of sin. Only the sovereign power of God is able to defend the Christian from the power of the devil, the world, and his own sinful flesh. Because God is sovereign, absolutely sovereign, the church's salvation is secure. The sovereignty of God gives the believer the assurance that "He which hath begun a good work in you will perform it until the day of Jesus Christ" (Phil. 1:6).

F. Relation to the five points

There is an intimate and necessary relationship between the sovereignty of God and its statement in the Five Points. To confess the Five Points of Calvinism is to confess the sovereignty of God. At the same time, there can be no belief in the Five Points apart from a strong belief in the sovereignty of God.

This can easily be seen by use of the acronym *TULIP*, dervied from the first letter of each of the Five Points: *T*otal depravity, *U*nconditional election, *L*imited atonement, *I*rresistible grace, and *P*erseverance of the saints. Because man is totally depraved, only the sovereign power of God can save him. Because God is sovereign, He chooses to save whom He wills to save, and there are no conditions or works men fulfill in order to earn their own salvation. Because God is sovereign, the atonement (redemption) accomplished by the death of Christ was effectual, actually saving those whom it was intended to save. Because God is sovereign, His gracious operations in the salvation of men are irresistible. Because God is sovereign, the saints personally, and the church as a whole, will be preserved, and as a result of that preservation will persevere to the end.

CHAPTER II

Total Depravity

The doctrine of total depravity is the first of the Five Points of Calvinism and is represented by the letter *T* in the memory-help *TULIP.*

In the Canons of Dordt, the original Five Points of Calvinism, total depravity is not the first point. Unconditional election, represented by the *U* of *TULIP,* is first. The reason for this is historical. At the time the Canons were written, it was the doctrine of unconditional election that was being attacked more than any other doctrine, and it was that doctrine, therefore, which was defended first.

There is good reason for putting total depravity first. Because the doctrine of total depravity describes man's sinfulness and wretched condition, it shows the *need* for the grace of God described in the other four points. We *must* see our need before we can have any appreciation for the grace of God that brings salvation. In other words, we must have a correct diagnosis of man's spiritual condition, as we do in the first of the Five Points, in order to see that the remedy prescribed by the other four points is the correct remedy. For this reason especially, it is best to begin with total depravity and not with unconditional election.

A. The doctrine
1. Depravity

This doctrine is sometimes called "total inability," emphasizing correctly sinful man's inability to do good. This label, however, is deficient in one respect. It describes man's wickedness only as a lack of good, forgetting that the opposite is also true. Sinful man not only lacks good but is actively and willingly evil. Since the word "depravity" emphasizes this, total depravity is the better name.

When we describe man's sinfulness as *depravity*, we are not just saying that he is bad or wicked, but that he is rebelliously and deliberately evil, that he loves and delights in wickedness of every kind. He is not just passively overcome by sin but actively and willingly uses his strength, ability, and gifts to sin.

The truth, then, is that men are very wicked, much more wicked than they themselves would ever admit. Nor is this wickedness incidental, but deeply imbedded in what a man is, what we call his "nature." In other words, his depravity is not something he has learned or that is the result of his environment, but he is by nature wicked. He does not just do evil but *is* evil. He is conceived and born a sinner.

The explanation for this is original sin. We refer to the sin of man in Adam and every man's responsibility for the sin that Adam committed. Adam did not stand in paradise as a private individual, his deeds having consequences for himself alone, but as the head and representative of us all. He was the king of the earthly creation. Being a king, what he did affected all those over whom he was king. The result was that when Adam sinned, we sinned. His sin was reckoned by God to be our sin. This is the clear teaching of Romans 5:12: "Wherefore, as by one man sin entered into the world, and death by sin; and so death passed upon all men, for that all have sinned." (See also 1 Cor. 15:22.)

The result was that the punishment of Adam's sin was visited by God upon all men. All men have sinned in Adam, and all men share in the punishment of that sin. That punishment was death. God's threat was, "For in the day that thou eatest thereof thou shalt surely die" (Gen. 2:17). God carried out that threat. Man died—God killed him. One aspect of that death is what the Bible refers to as *spiritual* death, the loss of man's spiritual life, his total depravity. God punished sin with sin.

So sinful is man by nature that he is *dead* in sin: "And you hath he quickened, who were dead in trespasses and sins" (Eph. 2:1). Man is not merely sick, very sick, even critically sick. He is dead. There is no spiritual life in him whatsoever. Being dead, he has no ability to raise himself to spiritual life, to cooperate in his spiritual resurrection, or even to desire it. From a human point of view, his condition is hopeless.

2. Total depravity

To speak of *total* depravity, then, is a bit redundant. We use this language, however, to emphasize that man is so wicked that he lacks any good, even the ability to do good or the desire to do what is good. This emphasis is necessary because of the many ways in which the doctrine of total depravity is denied.

Usually three things are meant by the word "total."

a. *Total* depravity means, first of all, that the *totality of the human race* is depraved. There is no one, not even a newborn infant, who is not corrupt and wicked. Nor are there any primitive people who still live in some kind of innocence. All are depraved.

b. *Total* depravity means also that *every part of man's*

      existence is filled with wickedness. In other words, not only his actions are wicked, but his speech, his thoughts, his motives, his wishes, his mind, his soul, his spirit—everything he is and does, inwardly and outwardly—are wicked. He cannot do, desire, or even understand what is good.

c.   *Total* depravity also means that every part of man's existence is *totally* wicked. That is to say, his mind is not partly wicked and partly good, but completely wicked. The same is true of every other part of his existence, especially of his will. His will, too, is in bondage, so that he cannot even want what is good, nor is there any desire for good to be found in his life and thoughts.

This does not mean that every man shows the evil of his sinful nature as much as possible and at all times. Not everyone has the opportunity or means to do so, or even the time in a brief life span. Also, God Himself puts various restraints on men to prevent them from doing all the wickedness that is in their hearts. Among these restraints are the fear of punishment, the desire for the approval of others, and the strictures of government and civil law. But it must be emphasized that these restraints are outward restraints only, something on the order of a muzzle on the jaws of a mad dog. They do not in any way lessen the actual wickedness of man or change his wicked heart or make it possible for him to do good. Man is, therefore, as bad as he can be, though he does not always show it and often hides it.

It must be remembered that this is not a judgment any man would make or want to make of himself or of others. Nor is this a judgment that can be made by observation. The reason for this is also to be found in man's depravity. Just as a blind man cannot fully understand his own blindness because he has never been able to see, so the sinner cannot comprehend his own sinfulness and always thinks well of himself (Jer. 17:9). The right judgment of man's spiritual state can only be made by God Himself. God makes that judgment in His Word and makes it by comparing men to the standard of His own holiness, not to any social standard or to other men. In fact, God's holiness and perfection are the only standard against which the doctrine of total depravity can be true, and we must learn the truth of total depravity from the Bible and not from our own observations of ourselves or of others.

B. Scripture proofs
1. References to total depravity
    a. Genesis 6:5: "And God saw that the wickedness of man was great in the earth, and that every imagination of the thoughts of his heart was only evil continually."

Notice the emphasis on the totality of man's depravity. When Scripture says that man's wickedness is "great," it explains this to mean "total" (*"every* imagination . . . *only* evil *continually"*). This is God's own judgment of man's condition ("God saw"). It may not be our judgment, and we may not agree with it, but that makes no difference.

    b. Genesis 8:21: "And the LORD smelled a sweet savour; and the LORD said in his heart, I will not again curse the ground any more for man's sake; for the imagination of man's heart is *evil from his youth;* neither will I again smite any more every thing living, as I have done."

Scripture once again records God's judgment of man's spiritual condition and this time shows that man's depravity is not merely something that belongs to his maturity but characterizes his life from its beginning.

> c. Job 15:14–16: "What is man, that he should be clean? and he which is born of a woman, that he should be righteous? Behold, he putteth no trust in his saints; yea, the heavens are not clean in his sight. How much more abominable and filthy is man, which drinketh iniquity like water."

In this text the Word of God reminds us that man's wickedness is as natural to him, and as much a part of his life, as drinking water. The emphasis is on God as the standard by which man is judged, even when man in his own sight may be clean.

> d. Psalm 14:1–3: "The fool hath said in his heart, There is no God. They are corrupt, they have done abominable works, there is *none* that doeth good. The LORD looked down from heaven upon the children of men, to see if there were any that did understand, and seek God. They are *all* gone aside, they are *all* together become filthy: there is *none* that doeth good, no, *not one*."

Depravity is here described as something that characterizes the whole human race. In that respect also it is *total*. Notice the fivefold emphasis on the fact that *no one* does any good. This is the judgment of God when He looks down on the human race. Our thinking must, then, be shaped by this Word of God and not by what we ourselves or anyone else may think.

> e. Jeremiah 4:22: "For my people is foolish, they have not known me; they are sottish children, and they

have *no understanding:* they are wise to do evil, but *to do good they have no knowledge."*

Depravity, according to this passage, is so great that even God's people of themselves do not know how to do good. It is great also in that man is depraved not only in his actions, but even in his mind, knowledge, and understanding.

    f.   Jeremiah 13:23: "Can the Ethiopian change his skin, or the leopard his spots? then may ye also do good, that are accustomed to do evil."

It is as impossible for man, in his own strength, to do any good as it is for him to change the color of his skin. That is the truth of total depravity—not just that man does not do good, but that he *cannot.* Thus, the passage teaches us that man's depravity is *natural* to him. He is born depraved in the same way that a leopard is born spotted, and an Ethiopian black.

    g.   Jeremiah 17:9, 10: "The heart is deceitful above all things, and *desperately wicked:* who can know it? I the LORD search the heart, I try the reins, even to give to every man according to his ways, and according to the fruit of his doings."

With these words God asserts His right as judge and gives His judgment, telling us that our depravity does not merely consist in outwardly wicked actions, but that it is a matter of our hearts. Because our hearts are the fountain of all our life (Prov. 4:23), and because that fountain itself is impure, it is impossible that anything clean or good should come forth from it. Because a man's heart is "desperately wicked," his "ways" and his "fruits" will also be found wicked.

h. John 3:3, 5: "Jesus answered and said unto him [Nicodemus], Verily, verily, I say unto thee, Except a man be born again, he *cannot* see the kingdom of God . . . Verily, verily, I say unto thee, Except a man be born of water and of the Spirit, he *cannot* enter the kingdom of God."

Jesus tells Nicodemus and us that we cannot even see (understand) the kingdom of God except by a miracle. That must be the miracle of a whole new life. As far as the life we now live is concerned, there is no hope. This, of course, is the *application* of the doctrine of total depravity that must be made. It is not just a doctrine, but a description of our hopeless condition as well.

i. John 6:44: "No man can come to me, except the Father which hath sent me draw him: and I will raise him up at the last day."

This verse is concerned with faith, described here as coming to Jesus. This coming to Jesus, or believing, Jesus says, is impossible except by the power of God. No man has that power of himself. This is especially important because so many Christians have the mistaken idea that believing is the one good action that sinful man can do. The Word of God says that this is not so.

j. John 12:37–40: "But though he had done so many miracles before them, yet they believed not on him: That the saying of Esaias [Isaiah] the prophet might be fulfilled, which he spake, Lord, who hath believed our report? and to whom hath the arm of the Lord been revealed? Therefore they *could not* believe, because that Esaias said again, He hath blinded their eyes, and hardened their heart; that they should not see with their eyes, nor understand with their heart, and be converted, and I should heal them."

Again the emphasis of Scripture is on man's total inability to believe apart from the grace of God, but we also find that this depravity of man is the direct result of God's judgment upon man and does not just happen to be the case with him. His depravity is, as we have seen, the spiritual death that God inflicted on him in the beginning (Gen. 2:17).

> k. Romans 1:28–32: "And even as they did not like to retain God in their knowledge, God gave them over to a reprobate mind, to do those things which are not convenient; Being filled with *all* unrighteousness, fornication, wickedness, covetousness, maliciousness; full of envy, murder, debate, deceit, malignity; whisperers, Backbiters, *haters of God,* despiteful, proud, boasters, inventors of evil things, disobedient to parents, Without understanding, covenant-breakers, without natural affection, implacable, unmerciful: Who knowing the judgment of God, that they which commit such things are worthy of death, not only do the same, but have pleasure in them that do them."

Once again the Word of God establishes the fact that man's will is not at all inclined toward God ("they did not like to retain God in their knowledge"), but toward evil. In fact, we read here that men not only do evil but delight in it, even though they know the judgment of God. The preceding context supports this fully by showing that the worship of the heathen is not a seeking after God or longing for him, but a changing of the truth of God into a lie.

l. Romans 3:9–19: "What then? are we better than they? No, in no wise: for we have before proved both Jews and Gentiles, that they are *all under sin;* As it is written, There is *none* righteous, no, not one: There is *none* that understandeth, there is *none* that seeketh after God. They are *all* gone out of the way, they are all together become unprofitable; there is *none* that doeth good, no, *not one.* Their throat is an open sepulchre; with their tongues they have used deceit; the poison of asps is under their lips: Whose mouth is full of cursing and bitterness: Their feet are swift to shed blood: Destruction and misery are in their ways: And the way of peace have they not known: There is no fear of God before their eyes. Now we know that what things soever the law saith, it saith to them who are under the law: that every mouth may be stopped, and *all the world may become guilty* before God."

The apostle Paul is quoting here from *eight* different Old Testament passages to prove the depravity of man. That, in itself, is a powerful testimony to the fact that all the Scriptures teach this doctrine. But he shows especially that all are under sin and that this is due to the fact that all are guilty before God. He also shows from the Scriptures that both in relation to God and to men, in understanding, speech, and deeds, man is wicked. The text, therefore, proves both the first and the third aspects of *total* depravity of which we spoke before.

m. Romans 6:16–19: "Know ye not, that to whom ye yield yourselves servants to obey, his servants ye are to whom ye obey; whether of sin unto death, or of obedience unto righteousness? But God be thanked, that ye were the servants of sin, but ye have obeyed from the heart that form of doctrine which was delivered you. Being then made free from sin, ye became the servants of righteousness. I speak after the manner of men because of the infirmity of your flesh: for as ye have yielded your members servants to uncleanness and to iniquity unto iniquity; even so now yield your members servants to righteousness unto holiness."

Paul now describes man's inability to do good as spiritual slavery, which indeed it is, for in sin we not only refuse to have God as our Master but give our members, that is, our bodies, to the service of sin and Satan. Having done so, we can no longer serve God.

n. Romans 8:7, 8: "Because the carnal mind is enmity against God: for it is not subject to the law of God, neither indeed can be. So then they that are in the flesh cannot please God."

Thus Scripture shows that man does not just do evil, perhaps without even intending it, but that he *is* evil and that his evil-doing is always conscious, active rebellion ("enmity") against God. Not only is he not subject to God and not pleasing to God, but he *cannot* be. He has no ability to do or to be good.

o. Galatians 3:22: "But the scripture hath concluded *all* under sin, that the promise by faith of Jesus Christ might be given to them that believe."

This is New Testament proof that sin is slavery, that depravity is total in the sense that it is true of all men, and that this is not our judgment of ourselves and others, but Scripture's judgment.

p. Ephesians 2:1, 5: "And you hath he quickened, who were *dead* in trespasses and sins; . . . Even when we were *dead* in sins, hath quickened us together with Christ, (by grace ye are saved)."

This time our depravity is described as a spiritual death to help us understand that no more than a dead man can think, will, understand, speak, or act can we think, will, understand, speak, or act in a way that is pleasing to God without grace and salvation. This passage is proof, therefore, that total depravity and spiritual death are one and the same.

q. Colossians 2:13: "And you, being *dead* in your sins and the uncircumcision of your flesh, hath he quickened together with him, having forgiven you all trespasses."

This verse reproduces Ephesians 2:1 and 5 almost word for word, but we should note the emphasis on the word "you" in both passages. Paul is reminding us that total depravity does not apply just to the heathen or to savages, but also to civilized, educated members of the church, such as these Colossians and ourselves.

r. Titus 3:3: "For we ourselves also were sometimes foolish, disobedient, deceived, serving divers lusts and pleasures, living in malice and envy, hateful, and hating one another."

Once more the emphasis lies on the fact that we must confess the truth of total depravity not just of men in general, or of other men, but of *ourselves*. Otherwise, depravity is not *total* depravity.

2. References to original sin
   a. Genesis 5:3: "And Adam lived an hundred and thirty years, and begat a son in his own likeness, after his image; and called his name Seth."

What a testimony this is against man who was created in the image of God but who now begets children, not in God's image, but in his own! We have seen in the preceding passages what that image is like.

   b. Job 14:4: "Who can bring a clean thing out of an unclean? not one."

Not only does this text teach that it is impossible for a sinner to produce anything good by his own words, thoughts, and actions, but it also shows that he cannot even produce offspring who are any different from himself. As the Canons of Dordt say, "A corrupt stock produced a corrupt offspring" (III/IV, 2).

   c. Psalm 51:5: "Behold, I was shapen in iniquity, and in sin did my mother conceive me."

Here we see the truth that wickedness is not something learned, but hereditary and original, attaching itself to the infant still within the womb. We should note, however, that "in sin" does not mean that the act of procreation is sinful, but that we are conceived and born utterly sinful, slaves of Satan. Our whole lives are "in sin."

   d. Psalm 58:3: "The wicked are estranged from the womb: they go astray as soon as they be born, speaking lies."

This text proves that even the depravity of infants is not just a lack of good but an inclination to evil action. One has only to observe small children to see that they know naturally how to tell lies and go astray from God. In fact, they can be taught to speak the truth and follow God only with great effort crowned by the grace of God.

> e. Romans 5:12: "Wherefore, as by one man sin entered into the world, and death by sin; and so death passed upon all men, for that all have sinned."

In this important verse Scripture teaches not only that spiritual death or depravity is hereditary, but that it is hereditary because all men have sinned and therefore are guilty in Adam. That is the doctrine of original sin and a reminder that man cannot be in any worse condition than he now is before God.

There are, of course, many other passages that could be quoted, but these are the principal ones, and they show that whatever people may think of the doctrine of total depravity, it is unmistakably the teaching of Scripture.

C. Difficult passages

A number of Scripture passages are used against the doctrine of total depravity. We should look at some of them and see what they actually teach. Thus, we will see clearly that the Scriptures do not contradict themselves or teach anything else than man's total depravity.

> 1. Deuteronomy 29:19: "And it come to pass, when he heareth the words of this curse, that he bless himself in his heart, saying, I shall have peace, though I walk in

the imagination of mine heart, to add drunkenness to thirst."

This verse would seem to teach that natural man (man un-saved) has a free will, that is, that he can *choose* whether or not he wants life or death, blessing or cursing, even though he may not be able to obtain these things by his own strength. If he can choose them, he can do real good, for there are few things as pleasing to God as choosing life and blessing.

The mistake that is made, however, is concluding that the *command* to choose between life and death implies that men have the *power* to obey it. That is not true. Natural man *cannot* obey anything God commands, but God continues to command it of him and judges him for his disobedience. Nor is it unfair of God to command what man cannot do, for it was man who willingly chose his own condition when he fell into sin in the beginning.

2. Joshua 24:15, 22: "And if it seem evil unto you to serve the LORD, choose you this day whom ye will serve; whether the gods which your fathers served that were on the other side of the flood, or the gods of the Amor-ites, in whose land ye dwell: but as for me and my house, we will serve the LORD . . . If ye forsake the LORD, and serve strange gods, then he will turn and do you hurt, and consume you, after that he hath done you good."

This is another passage that might seem to teach that people not only have the *opportunity* to choose either the service of God or idolatry, but are actually *able* by themselves to choose the service of God. If it is true that men can choose to serve God by the power of their own wills (choosing being the ac-tivity of the will), then they are able to do some good and can-not be said to be *totally* depraved.

The solution to this must be found in the context, especially in verse 19, where Joshua tells the people that they *cannot* serve the Lord. The text does not mean, however, that God's people, those who are saved by God's grace, cannot choose to serve God. They do, and they not only *choose* to serve Him but actually *do* serve Him, though never without sin. They can do good, but *only* because God Himself has worked in them both to will and to do His good pleasure (Phil. 2:13). Apart from God's grace, Joshua's words remain always true: "Ye *cannot* serve the Lord."

> 3. 2 Kings 10:28, 30: "Thus Jehu destroyed Baal out of Israel . . . And the LORD said unto Jehu, Because thou hast done well in executing that which is right in mine eyes, and hast done unto the house of Ahab according to all that was in mine eyes, and hast done unto the house of Ahab according to all that was in mine heart, thy children of the fourth generation shall sit on the throne of Israel."

The argument is that Jehu, though he himself was a wicked man, was nevertheless able to do good by doing what God had commanded when he destroyed the whole family of wicked Ahab. It is very clear, however, that Jehu did not do this out of love for God, for he himself reestablished the worship of the golden calves, which Jeroboam had originally set up to keep the people from the worship of God in Jerusalem (1 Kings 12:26–30). Instead, he did what God commanded only for himself and to secure the kingdom for himself. The Bible teaches us that whatever is not done for the glory of God, even though it be what God commands, is neither obedience nor good in the sight of God (Matt. 22:37, 38; Matt. 23:25–28; Rom. 14:23; 1 Cor. 10:31).

4. Acts 2:40: "And with many other words did he testify and exhort, saying, *Save yourselves* from this untoward generation."

The command to the people gathered for Pentecost to save themselves does not imply that they have the ability to do that. In fact, the Word of God makes it very clear that no man has that power in himself (Eph. 2:8–10).

5. Acts 16:31: "And they said, Believe on the Lord Jesus Christ, and thou shalt be saved, and thy house."

What we have just said applies to faith also. The *command* to believe does not imply that all men who hear that command have the *ability* to obey or that their believing depends upon their choosing whether or not they will do it. Ephesians 2:8–10 emphatically says that faith is a gift of God, not man's own work.

6. Romans 2:14, 15: "For when the Gentiles, which have not the law, do by nature the things contained in the law, these, having not the law, are a law unto themselves: Which shew the work of the law written in their hearts, their consciences also bearing witness, and their thoughts the mean while accusing or else excusing one another."

Though these verses say that the Gentiles, that is, the heathen, do the works of the law and have the work of the law written in their hearts, they do not say that this is in any way good in the sight of God. Actually, the opposite is true: they are all *under sin* (Rom. 3:9), and their doing the works of the law is their condemnation and leaves them without excuse (Rom. 1:19,

20). The context, then, makes it clear that this passage does not at all contradict the truth of total depravity, but supports it.

Many other passages could be cited in this connection, but the main points are clear. The commands of God do not imply that man has the power to obey them. Nor is mere outward conformity to the law of God *good* in God's eyes, but instead a great abomination.

D. Objections
   1. "Total depravity is a depressing doctrine."

One objection to the doctrine of total depravity is that it destroys people's happiness and peace and leads to unhappiness or worse. If this is true, the doctrine cannot possibly be biblical, for the teaching of the Bible is designed to be "good news" and to lead to the greatest happiness and blessing (Ps. 29:11; Ps. 119:165; 2 Cor. 1:3, 4).

The objection overlooks the fact that the doctrine of total depravity is never preached apart from the other doctrines of grace. Those doctrines of grace and salvation are God's remedy for our depravity and bring us all joy.

The divine "diagnosis" of total depravity must precede the application of the proper remedy to the sinner. Without such a correct diagnosis, the remedy will never be recognized or received. The Scriptures themselves show this. In Luke 5:32 Jesus says, "I came not to call the righteous [that is, those who think that they are righteous], but sinners [that is, those who know themselves to be sinners] to repentance." The parable of the Pharisee and the publican was specifically addressed to "certain which trusted in themselves that they were righteous, and despised others" (Luke 18:9). In that parable the man who acknowledged himself a sinner went home justified. The Pharisee, who did not know himself to be totally depraved, did not.

2. "Total depravity contradicts our experience."

Another objection sometimes adduced against the biblical teaching of total depravity is that it contradicts our experience. People just do not appear to be as bad as the Bible seems to indicate they are. This is apparently even more of a problem when one looks at the "good" deeds, the works of charity and philanthropy, that people do.

We must remember several things in answering this objection. First, we must remember that even our ability to see and judge sin is affected by our own sinfulness. One of the characteristics of the sinner is that he is spiritually *blind,* not just to his own sin, but also to the sinfulness of mankind. His heart deceives him also in this (Jer. 17:9).

We need to remember, too, that we see only the outward deeds a person does. We cannot see his heart and cannot, therefore, know anything about his motives in doing works of charity and philanthropy. And the Word says that anything not done out of faith, with thanks and for the glory of God, is *sin* (Isa. 66:3; Rom. 1:20, 21; Rom. 14:23; 1 Cor. 10:31).

What is more, when our experience seems to contradict the Word of God at this or any point, there is no question what we must believe. The Word of God must stand, and before it even our experience must bow.

E. Denials of total depravity

In the history of the church there have been many attacks on the doctrine of total depravity and many different ways in which the doctrine has been denied. It is good to know something about these errors, because they are still being taught today. We will study them, however, not by way of criticizing any particular person who may believe differently, but so that we ourselves may be firmly grounded in the truth (Col. 2:7).

1. Pelagianism

The oldest of the heresies that denies total depravity is the error of Pelagianism, named after the British monk who first taught it in the fifth century. This error is mentioned seven times by name in the Canons of Dordt.

Pelagianism teaches that Adam's sin had *no* consequences for his descendants and therefore all men are born spiritually neutral, neither good nor bad. Thus it is possible that they live an entirely sinless life. Even having sinned, according to Pelagius, it is possible for man to return to harmony with God by his own will and good works, and if he receives God's grace, it is only an assisting grace, not a grace that is efficacious (powerful unto salvation). The fact that most men *are* sinners is to be explained only by their imitating others and not by any inherent or natural tendency toward sin.

This error is still taught today in many forms. It is really the error that lies behind modern educational philosophy, modern psychology and psychiatry, and modern judicial theory. These all hold that man's only problem is that he learns (by imitation or from his environment) wrong patterns of behavior, which must be changed and can be changed by education, rehabilitation, or psychiatric counseling. A very good example of this philosophy is the modern idea that criminals ought not be punished but rehabilitated. This, of course, is humanism through and through, but Pelagianism and humanism are really the same thing. In both cases sin is not seen as sin against God; the total depravity of man is not recognized, and man's faults are only viewed as social failures.

The chief problem, however, is that much of the church world has accepted this humanistic and Pelagian philosophy. It is taught, for example, by those who advocate a "self-help" gospel, or a gospel of "positive thinking," which teaches that man is basically good, must not think guilty thoughts, and can save himself by his own willpower. It is accepted by those who see the calling of the church not as the calling to preach the gospel, but to do away with slums, poverty, sickness, segregation, and other such social evils, in other words, to change man's bad environment. It is part of the notion that the church's fight is the fight against earthly oppression. It is the essence of so-called liberation theology that salvation consists in the liberation of all the poor and oppressed peoples of the world.

All such teaching is Pelagian in that it does not recognize man's spiritually fallen condition and believes that he is fully able to help himself and deliver himself from his problems. In addition, of course, there is a Pelagian tendency in all of us in that we often fail to see our own sin and its seriousness and try so often to find our own way out of our sin problems. That is the real reason why Pelagianism is so dangerous.

2. Semi-Pelagianism

Semi-Pelagianism is a modified form of Pelagianism that was taught in the church after Augustine. Due to Augustine's influence the church first rejected Pelagianism, but later compromised and began to teach what is called Semi-Pelagianism. Semi-Pelagianism is still today the theology of the Roman Catholic Church.

Semi-Pelagianism says that Adam's fall *did* have an effect upon Adam's descendants and that they *are* born sinners. However, Semi-Pelagianism teaches that the effect of Adam's fall is not that men are totally depraved, or *dead* in sin, but that they are only *sick* in sin. In other words, man still has some ability to do good, just as a sick man still has some power to help himself. Semi-Pelagianism teaches that man is so sick in sin that though he can do good, he cannot actually save himself. Nevertheless, apart from saving grace he *is able* to do good works and to earn some favor with God (the Roman Catholic doctrine of meritorious good works). God helps men do good by giving them all "prevenient grace," that is, grace that makes it possible for them to do good and to merit without having received saving grace.

3. Arminianism

Arminianism is a further modification of Semi-Pelagianism that is taught in Protestant circles. Like Pelagianism, it is named after the man who first taught it, Jacobus Arminius. It was against his heresy that the Canons of Dordt were written. For a good understanding of Arminianism one should consult the negative (Rejection of Errors) sections of the Canons. Arminianism is different from Pelagianism only in this respect: it rejects the idea that men can do all sorts of meritorious good works and teaches that there is but *one* good thing that he can do by his own power, the good work of choosing Christ or of believing in Him. In other words, the principal teaching of Arminianism is that man has a free will and that he is not totally the slave of sin. It teaches that man's will is hindered by sin, but that God gives grace to all men sufficient to remove these hindrances so that men can, by their own power, choose for or against God. The difference, then, between Roman Catholic Semi-Pelagianism and Protestant Arminianism is that in Semi-Pelagianism salvation is of him that *runneth* (worketh), and in Arminianism it is of him that *willeth* (chooseth) (Rom. 9:16). In neither case is it *of God* who shows mercy.

Arminianism is, by and large, the belief of the majority of Christians today. The whole theology, for example, of "decisions for Christ," of "accepting Christ," of "opening one's heart to Christ," of the altar call, and of the "Jesus is waiting" type of preaching, presupposes that man has yet some ability and freedom of will and can do something in order to be saved. Faith, then, is not a gift of God, but man's own good work.

It is not difficult to see that this is not the doctrine of total depravity. Nor is this merely an abstract doctrinal issue. This teaching, among other things, changes the very character of gospel preaching so that the preaching becomes an attempt to *sell* Christ to men and to persuade them to accept Him by their own free will, instead of a proclamation of the glory and grace of God.

4. Common grace

The teaching of a common grace of God also denies total depravity. It admits that man has no power to do what is called saving good, that is, the good of choosing for God, for Christ, and for salvation. It says, however, that there is a certain grace of God given to all men, even to the unsaved, that makes it possible for them to do what is called "civil good." Civil good, supposedly, refers to actions which have no saving value, but are, nevertheless, good in the sight of God in that they promote decency and good order in society and allow men to live in peace and harmony among themselves. Along with this, the doctrine of common grace usually teaches that there is a universal operation of the Holy Spirit in the hearts of all men that makes it possible for them to do this good and that keeps them from being as bad as they might be.

This is really no different from Arminianism in that it says there is still some good in man. It may be very little. It may be only civil good, but it is still good. Obviously, if man can do anything good, he is not *totally* wicked. It should also be pointed out, though, that this teaching fails to take into account the fact that there is more to a good deed than just the outward action. The most important thing is not the action itself but the *motivation* for it. If it is not done for God's glory and by faith, it is sin and God hates it (Prov. 21:4; Isa. 66:2, 3; Mal. 2:11–13).

5. The free offer of the gospel

This very common teaching says that the preaching of the gospel constitutes a well-intentioned offer from God to all who hear. God, for His part, wants their salvation and even offers it to them in the gospel, so it is said.

Apart from the fact that the Scriptures never once speak of the gospel as an offer of salvation, and apart from the inconsistency of believing this and at the same time saying that God from eternity does *not* want the salvation of all who hear the gospel, there is the fact that an offer, if it is to be meaningful, must be made to people who have some power to accept or refuse that offer. If man has any power to respond to an offer of grace in the gospel, he cannot be totally depraved. An offer of assistance to a dead man is meaningless, and an offer to teach physics to a monkey would be mere mockery. God's work is neither meaningless nor mockery.

The answer of many to this dilemma is to say that God gives to all men who hear the gospel a certain preparatory grace or common grace (another version of that doctrine) to make such a choice, but this is simply the old Roman Catholic doctrine and a denial of the biblical truth that grace is always irresistible and saving.

6. Free will

Many Christians today believe that man has a free will, that he is able to choose between good and evil, between God and the devil, between salvation and damnation. This is the basic teaching of Arminianism but is important enough that it should be mentioned separately. Nor is it much different from the idea that the gospel is an offer of grace. This freedom of the will, according to those who believe in it, may be limited, so that the sinner can do nothing more than make the necessary choice. God must do the rest. Yet it ascribes some ability to do good to fallen man, no matter how limited and small that ability may be. Free will and total depravity, therefore, are not only incompatible, but opposite doctrines.

7. Absolute depravity

Some make a distinction between what they call *total depravity* and something they call *absolute depravity*. Absolute depravity, so they say, is the doctrine we have been describing: that man is utterly bad, without any good or possibility of good to be found in him. That teaching, according to them, is neither Calvinistic nor biblical. *Total* depravity, in their opinion, means that men are wicked in every part—heart, soul, mind, and strength—but not completely wicked in any part. One writer uses the example of a few drops of ink in water. Every drop is discolored, but none is *completely* black. That, supposedly, is total depravity and the teaching of Scripture. Apart from the fact that this is mere sophistry (What is the difference between total and absolute?), it cannot be said to be the doctrine of total depravity, since it is not *total*. Nor is it the doctrine of depravity that has been taught by Reformed and Presbyterian churches from the time of the Reformation. Absolute depravity, if it refers to anything, refers to the depravity of the fallen angels *for whom there is no hope of salvation.*

F. Practical importance

There are many practical implications of the doctrine of total depravity. It is important that we see some of these implications so that we are persuaded that this doctrine is not a mere abstraction and so that debate about it is not just empty talk.

1. Total depravity and repentance

The most important practical implication of total depravity for each individual Christian is that knowledge of this doctrine leads to true repentance for sin. Only if we understand that we have no goodness at all and that we are entirely without hope, will we be able to see the greatness of our sin and mourn over it as we should. As long as we think there is even the least bit of good in us, we will not be inclined to think of our sins or confess them before God.

The opposite is also true. One who does not confess his sins daily before God and mourn for them does not really understand the truth of total depravity, even though he may call himself a Calvinist. Indeed, it may be said that the proof of our belief in total depravity is our attitude toward our own sins.

2. Total depravity and parental discipline

In our families it is the doctrine of total depravity that motivates faithful discipline of our children. When we constantly cover up and overlook the sins of our children, make excuses for them, and do not discipline our children as we should, it is because we do not take their sin seriously. If we do not take their sin seriously, it can be only because we fail to see that they are totally depraved.

The Bible itself makes this connection between the depravity of our children and the necessity of Christian parental discipline in Proverbs 23:13, 14: "Withhold not correction from the child: for if thou beatest him with the rod, *he shall not die.* Thou shalt beat him with the rod, and shalt *deliver his soul from hell.*" Clearly, only the parent who really believes that his child is hellbound in his sins will be able to receive the Word of God in these verses and obey it.

3. Total depravity and the gospel

In the church and on the mission field, only the faithful preaching of total depravity will convict the sinner of his need for the cross and insure at the same time that all the glory of his salvation is given to God. We all know from our own experience that as long as we have any strength or resources of our own, we do not turn for help to Christ as we should, and neither will the unconverted sinner as long as he is told that he has some worthiness or goodness of his own. Also, to the extent that the doctrine of total depravity is neglected in the preaching and some good is ascribed to the sinner, the honor and glory of God as the only Savior are stolen from Him.

The doctrine of total depravity, then, can never be a dangerous doctrine in the preaching of the true gospel, as some think, but it is an integral part of the gospel. The wonder of our own depravity and the wonder of salvation by grace go hand in hand. We cannot confess one without the other.

4. Total depravity and the antithesis

In the world and in relation to wicked men, only the truth of total depravity will motivate us to maintain our spiritual separation from the world (sometimes called the "antithesis"). If we think that there is any good in the ungodly, we will not see any reason to be separate from them. Only when we see that they are "unrighteousness," "darkness," "sons of Belial," "infidels," and "idolaters" will we heed the call to "come out from among them and be separate" (2 Cor. 6:14–17). Then and only then we will see that there is no possibility of cooperating with them (2 Chron. 19:2), intermarrying with them (2 Cor. 6:14), or keeping fellowship with them (Eph. 5:11).

These are some of the more important implications of the doctrine for our life. May we see in them the importance of holding to this doctrine without compromise or neglect.

G. Relation to the other four points

A close relationship exists between this first point and the other four points. There are those who call themselves three- or four-point Calvinists and even hold to some degree to these truths, but in the end, because these five truths are so closely interwoven with each other, it is impossible to maintain any of them consistently without maintaining them all.

The relationship is this: the doctrine of total depravity makes sovereign grace the only possible way of salvation. It requires an *election* that is unconditional, not depending on man's work or worthiness; an *atonement* that does not just make salvation possible for all men, but actually saves those whom God has chosen; and a *grace* that is so powerful as to be utterly irresistible and that saves to the uttermost those who receive it, so that they are preserved and do persevere to the end.

CHAPTER III

Unconditional Election

The doctrine of unconditional election is the second of the Five Points of Calvinism. It is represented by the letter *U* in the acronym *TULIP.* Election and reprobation are the two parts of the larger doctrine of predestination.

The doctrine of predestination has been called the heart of the gospel. This is true. The gospel is the good news of salvation, and those who are saved are those whom God has predestined unto salvation, namely, the elect. The gospel declares the suffering and death of Jesus Christ for unworthy sinners, but Christ died only for those unworthy sinners who have been chosen by God. The gospel calls men to faith in Jesus Christ, but faith is worked only in the hearts of the elect. The preaching of the gospel is the means to gather the church. Those who are members of the church—genuine church members in God's eyes—constitute the *elect.*

It is imperative that every believer have a good understanding of predestination. There is much ignorance and confusion over this doctrine in our day. Besides, there are numerous corruptions and denials of this doctrine in places where historically it was confessed. Many are abandoning the doctrine because they are deceived into supposing that it is the invention of clever theologians and that it is not taught in the Scriptures. Others, who will admit that predestination is taught in the Bible, consider that it is a doctrine of little or no practical benefit for the church. These people are seriously mistaken! We must see that the doctrine of predestination (election and reprobation) is clearly taught in the Word of God, and we must be convinced that it is a doctrine of the greatest practical value for Christians.

We echo the sentiments of John Calvin: "Let those roar at us who will. We will ever brighten forth, with all our power of language, the doctrine which we hold concerning the free election of God, seeing that it is only by it that the faithful can understand how great that goodness of God is which effectually called them to salvation . . . Now, if we are not really ashamed of the Gospel, we must of necessity acknowledge what is therein openly declared: that God by His eternal goodwill . . . appointed those whom He pleased unto salvation, rejecting all the rest."[1]

Predestination is God's eternal decision before the beginning of the world (*pre-*) with respect to the everlasting destiny (*destination*) of all His rational, moral creatures: men, angels, and devils. There are many who become uneasy when the word predestination is mentioned, but predestination is not some hideous monster invented by theologians gone over the edge. The Bible teaches predestination.

The Greek word from which our English word "predestination" is derived occurs six times in the New Testament. We find it used twice by the apostle Paul in Romans 8:29, 30: "For whom he did foreknow, he also did *predestinate* to be conformed to the image of his Son, that he might be the firstborn among many brethren. Moreover whom he did *predestinate,* them he also called: and whom he called, them he also justified: and whom he justified, them he also glorified." In Ephesians 1:5 the apostle Paul describes God's choice of the elect in these words: "Having *predestinated* us unto the adoption of children by Jesus Christ to himself, according to the good pleasure of his will." And we read in Ephesians 1:11 of Christ, "in whom also we have obtained an inheritance, being *pre-*

destinated according to the purpose of him who worketh all things after the counsel of his own will."

The word predestination is also found in Acts 4:28, where it is translated as "determined before." There the apostle Peter teaches that Christ's crucifixion and the role in Christ's crucifixion played by wicked Herod and Pontius Pilate were predestined by God. In that context he declares in verse 28 that these wicked rulers were gathered together "to do whatsoever thy [God's] hand and thy counsel determined before [predestined] to be done."

In 1 Corinthians 2:7 the word predestinate is translated "ordained": "But we speak the wisdom of God in a mystery, even the hidden wisdom, which God *ordained* [predestined] before the world unto our glory." Here Paul teaches that the whole plan of salvation was predestined by God.

The Reformed faith maintains the biblical doctrine of "double predestination," that is, not only election, but also *reprobation.* God's election of men in Jesus Christ is selective and discriminating. Not all men are chosen by God and appointed to salvation. In reality, many are excluded and rejected. In the words of the Canons of Dordt, I, Article 15, "What peculiarly tends to illustrate and recommend to us the eternal and unmerited grace of election, is the express testimony of sacred Scripture, that not all, but some only are elected, while others are passed by in the eternal decree." This is the teaching of reprobation, which we will discuss further under heading B. The remainder of this chapter will illustrate God's sovereignty in predestination (election and reprobation) in more specific detail.

A. The doctrine of election

By election we mean the eternal choice by God of certain definite individuals in Jesus Christ unto salvation.

There are many references in the Scriptures to this election or choice by God. It is the Lord Jesus who declares in Matthew 22:14, "Many are called, but few are *chosen* [elect]." In Romans 11:5 the apostle Paul writes, "Even so then at this present time also there is a remnant according to the *election* of grace." The same apostle writes in Ephesians 1:4, "According as he hath *chosen* [elected] us in him before the foundation of the world." In Colossians 3:12 he calls believers to "Put on therefore, as the *elect* of God, holy and beloved, bowels of mercies, kindness, humbleness of mind, meekness, longsuffering." In Titus 1:1 reference is made to ". . . the faith of God's *elect*." The apostle Peter writes in 1 Peter 2:9, "But ye are a *chosen* [elect] generation, a royal priesthood, an holy nation." And in 2 Peter 1:10 he exhorts Christians, "Wherefore the rather, brethren, give diligence to make your calling and *election* sure."

The outstanding characteristics of election include the following:

1. Decretive

Election is a decree, a decision or choice of God. God elects, and God elects whom He wills to elect. Election is part of the counsel and will of God. In Romans 8:29, 30 we read, "Whom he [God] did *foreknow*, he also did predestinate." In Ephesians 1:4 we read, "According as he [God] *hath chosen*." Ephesians 1:11 states, "In whom we have obtained an inheritance, being predestinated *according to the purpose of him [God] who worketh all things after the counsel of his [God's] own will*."

2. Personal

Election is God's choice of certain *definite individuals*. Election is not a vague and indefinite decree of God that merely determines that there shall be salvation, nor is it a decision on the part of God to save simply a mass of human beings. Instead, election is God's determination to save particular persons. Ephesians 1:4 teaches this: "According as he hath chosen *us.*" In John 15:16 Jesus says, "Ye have not chosen me, but I have chosen *you,* and ordained *you.*" In Romans 9:11–13 the apostle Paul teaches that Jacob, a definite individual, was elected by God, while Esau, a definite individual, was not elected by God.

3. Eternal

Election is the *eternal* choice of God of certain persons. Election does not take place in time and history as God's response to the actions of men, but election is eternal election. Again we quote Paul in Ephesians 1:4: "According as he hath chosen us in him *before the foundation of the world.*" The apostle John speaks in Revelation 17:8 of those "whose names were written in the book of life *from the foundation of the world.*"

4. Unto salvation

The purpose of election is the salvation of those persons whom God has eternally chosen. They are not chosen merely to some earthly, temporal privileges, but they are chosen unto salvation itself. In Romans 8:30 those who are predestinated are justified (have their sins forgiven and Christ's righteousness imputed to them) and are glorified (go to heaven). Paul teaches in Ephesians 1:5 that we are predestinated "unto the adoption of children by Jesus Christ to himself." In Revelation 17:8 the elect are said to have their names written in the book of life, that is, everlasting life, life with God in the perfection of the new heavens and earth.

5. Gracious

That a person is elected by God is not due to anything in that person but is due to the free, unmerited grace of God. The cause of election is not at all to be found in those who are elected, but lies only in the will of the electing God. Those who are elected are no different or better in themselves than those who are not elected. All men, as was made plain in the previous chapter, are by nature dead in trespasses and sins. That some men, in distinction from others, should be chosen by God to salvation is to be attributed solely to the grace of God. Paul writes in Ephesians 2:8, "For *by grace* are ye saved through faith; and that not of yourselves: it is the gift of God." In Romans 11:5 he speaks of "a remnant according to the election *of grace.*"

6. Unconditional

If election is gracious, it follows that it must also be unconditional. If election is due *alone* to the grace of God, it is not *conditioned* upon anything in man or that man must do. This is a crucial point! There are many who profess to hold to biblical election but who deny the truth of election by making election conditional. This was the false teaching concerning election propounded by the Arminians at the Synod of Dordt. The Arminians professed to believe in election, but the election that they taught was a conditional election. According to this view, God in eternity looked into the future and saw who would believe on Him and who would choose Him. These, in turn, God chose and elected as His people. Election became God's choosing those who had chosen Him. However, this conception of election cannot stand the test of Scripture. Speaking of God's election of Jacob and rejection of Esau, Paul writes in Romans 9:11, "For the children being not yet born, neither having done any good or evil, that the purpose of God according to election might stand, *not of works,* but of him that calleth." The Lord Jesus teaches unconditional election in the clearest of language in John 15:16: "Ye have not chosen me, but I have chosen you, and ordained you." Jesus does not mean to teach here that we do not choose Him. We do choose Jesus Christ. We do desire salvation. We do willingly follow Him as His disciples. But Jesus' concern here is with who chose first and whose choice is decisive. His teaching in John 15:16 is that we choose Him only because of, and as the result of, His choice of us. Our choice of Him is not the reason for His choice of us; rather, His choice of us is the explanation of our choice of Him. His choice of us is not dependent on our choice of Him; our choice of Him is dependent on His choice of us.

The Bible also teaches unconditional election when it sets forth the truth that our good works, faith, and repentance are not the cause or reason why God has chosen us, but are the fruit, result, and evidence of our election. Many passages of Scripture establish this relationship between God's election and our works. In John 15:16 Jesus says that He has chosen us not because we have shown fruit, but *so that* we should go and bring forth fruit. Paul writes in Ephesians 1:4 that God has chosen us not because of our holiness, but "*that* we should be holy and without blame." He writes in Ephesians 2:10, "For we are his workmanship, created in Christ Jesus *unto* [not "because of"] good works, which God hath before ordained that we should walk in them." Not only is it taught that we are chosen *unto* good works, but there is added the statement that these works themselves have been ordained for us by God.

7. In Jesus Christ

Although there is no basis for God's election in those who are elected, there *is* a basis for their election. That basis is to be found alone in Jesus Christ and in His suffering and death as the Son of God. Not *our* worth but the worth of Christ is the basis for God's election of us. Not *our* works but the work of Christ is the ground. There must be a basis for God's election of those who are in themselves totally depraved, guilty sinners. That basis for their election, as for all of their salvation, is in Jesus Christ. In Ephesians 1:4 we read, "According as he [God] hath chosen us *in him* [Jesus Christ]." And in verse 5 of the same chapter he writes, "Having predestinated us unto the adoption of children *by Jesus Christ.*"

B. The doctrine of reprobation

Like election, reprobation is an eternal decree of God. According to this decree God appoints certain definite persons to the everlasting destiny of rejection and damnation in hell. Those so reprobated deserve this punishment to which they are appointed because of their unbelief and other sins, for God does not owe salvation to them nor to anyone.

Reprobation demonstrates the sovereignty of God in salvation in that God does what He wills with the creatures He has made. In and of themselves, the reprobate are not worse than the elect. All men appear in the mind of God as involved in a common ruin. The ultimate explanation of God's electing some and reprobating others is His own sovereign good pleasure. Jesus says, "Even so, Father, for so it seemed good in thy sight" (Matt. 11:26). Beyond that we cannot go, and before this revealed truth we humans must bow. Theoretically, God could have chosen to save all men (for He has the power to do so), or He could have chosen to save none (for He was under no obligation to save any). But He did neither. Instead, He has chosen to save some and exclude others.

The first proof for reprobation is the Greek word, inspired

by the Holy Spirit in the New Testament, that is translated "elect" or "chosen" in our King James Version of the Bible. That Greek word means literally "to choose *out of*," not simply "to choose." This clearly implies reprobation. If God's elect are chosen out of the fallen human race, it follows that there are others out of whom the elect have been chosen. These others have not been chosen; they are the non-elect, or reprobate.

The truth of reprobation also follows necessarily from election. Even the enemies of the doctrine of predestination have recognized this. Repeatedly they have charged that reprobation is only a logical deduction that is made from the truth of election, a logical deduction, according to them, that is not necessarily in harmony with reality. We intend to show that reprobation is not *simply* a logical implication of election but the express teaching of the Scriptures as well, even as the Reformed faith has always maintained. It certainly is true that reprobation follows logically from the truth of election. One cannot consistently hold to election without also confessing reprobation. Neither can one deny reprobation without, by that very fact, denying election also. Since election is God's choice of definite, particular persons, it follows that there are those who are not so chosen by God. Those who deny reprobation but make some effort to still hold to election are forced to teach an election according to which God chooses *all* men and desires the salvation of *all* men. Then there is no particular election. The reason, they say, why some men in distinction from others are in the end actually saved is due to those men themselves, to their free will and to their good works. Thus the unconditionality of election is denied. Election is no longer God's gracious election. History, too, has demonstrated—let men open their eyes!—that the denial of reprobation is inherently an attack upon and a rejection of unconditional election.

C. Scripture proofs for election

References to a body of people, the church, whom God saves are found throughout the Bible.

1. The Old Testament

The outstanding example of election in the Old Testament is God's election of the nation of Israel. In distinction from all other nations, God chose Israel to be His people:

    a. Deuteronomy 7:6: "For thou art an holy people unto the Lord thy God: the Lord thy God hath *chosen* thee to be a special people unto himself, above all people that are upon the face of the earth."

    b. 1 Kings 3:8: "And thy servant [Solomon] is in the midst of thy people which thou hast *chosen,* a great people, that cannot be numbered nor counted for multitude."

    c. Psalm 105:6: "O ye seed of Abraham his servant, ye children of Jacob his *chosen.*"

    d. Psalm 132:13: "For the Lord hath *chosen* Zion; he hath desired it for his habitation."

    e. Isaiah 41:8: "But thou, Israel, art my servant, Jacob whom I have *chosen,* the seed of Abraham my friend."

    f. Isaiah 45:4: "For Jacob my servant's sake, and Israel mine *elect,* I have even called thee [King Cyrus] by thy name: I have surnamed thee, though thou hast not known me."

2. The New Testament
    a. Matthew 22:14: "For many are called, but few are *chosen.*"

b. Matthew 24:31: "And he shall send his angels with a great sound of a trumpet, and they shall gather together his *elect* from the four winds, from one end of heaven to the other."

c. Mark 13:20: "And except that the Lord had shortened those days, no flesh should be saved: but for the *elect's* sake, whom he hath *chosen,* he hath shortened the days."

d. Luke 18:7: "And shall not God avenge his own *elect,* which cry day and night unto him, though he bear long with them?"

e. John 13:18: "I speak not of you all: I know whom I have *chosen:* but that the scripture might be fulfilled, He that eateth bread with me hath lifted up his heel against me."

f. John 15:16: "Ye have not chosen me, but I have *chosen* you, and *ordained* you, that ye should go and bring forth fruit, and that your fruit should remain: that whatsoever ye shall ask of the Father in my name, he may give it you."

g. John 17:9: "I pray for them: I pray not for the world, but for *them which thou hast given me;* for they are thine."

h. Romans 8:28–30: "And we know that all things work together for good to them that love God, to *them who are the called according to his purpose.* For whom he did foreknow [love in Christ], he also did *predestinate* to be conformed to the image of his Son, that he might be the firstborn among many brethren. Moreover whom he did *predestinate,* them he also called: and whom he called, them he also justified: and whom he justified, them he also glorified."

    i.   Romans 8:33: "Who shall lay any thing to the charge of God's *elect?*"

    j.   Romans 9:11–13: "(For the children being not yet born, neither having done any good or evil, that the purpose of God according to *election* might stand, not of works, but of him that calleth;) It was said unto her, The elder shall serve the younger. As it is written, Jacob have I loved, but Esau have I hated."

    k.   Romans 9:23: "And that he might make known the riches of his glory on the vessels of mercy, which he had *afore prepared* unto glory."

    l.   Romans 11:5: "Even so at this present time also there is a remnant according to the *election* of grace."

    m.   Romans 11:7: "What then? Israel hath not obtained that which he seeketh for but the *election* hath obtained it, and the rest were blinded."

    n.   Ephesians 1:3–5: "Blessed be the God and Father of our Lord Jesus Christ, who hath blessed us with all spiritual blessings in heavenly places in Christ: According as he hath *chosen* us in him before the foundation of the world, that we should be holy and without blame before him in love: Having *predestinated* us unto the adoption of children by Jesus Christ to himself, according to the good pleasure of his will."

    o.   Ephesians 1:11: "In whom also we have obtained an inheritance, being *predestinated* according to the purpose of him who worketh all things after the counsel of his own will."

    p.   Colossians 3:12: "Put on therefore, as the *elect* of God, holy and beloved, bowels of mercies, kindness, humbleness of mind, meekness, longsuffering."

q. 1 Thessalonians 1:4: "Knowing, brethren beloved, your *election* of God."

r. 1 Thessalonians 5:9: "For God hath not *appointed* us to wrath, but to obtain salvation by our Lord Jesus Christ."

s. 2 Thessalonians 2:13: "But we are bound to give thanks alway to God for you, brethren beloved of the Lord, because God hath from the beginning *chosen* you to salvation through sanctification of the Spirit and belief of the truth."

t. 2 Timothy 2:10: "Therefore I endure all things for the *elect's* sakes, that they may also obtain the salvation which is in Christ Jesus with eternal glory."

u. Titus 1:1: "Paul, a servant of God, and an apostle of Jesus Christ, according to the faith of God's *elect*."

v. 1 Peter 1:2: "*Elect* according to the foreknowledge of God the Father, through sanctification of the Spirit, unto obedience and sprinkling of the blood of Jesus Christ."

w. 1 Peter 2:9: "But ye are a *chosen* generation, a royal priesthood, an holy nation, a peculiar people; that ye should shew forth the praises of him who hath called you out of darkness into his marvellous light."

x. 1 Peter 5:13: "The church that is at Babylon, *elected* together with you, saluteth you; and so doth Marcus my son."

y. 2 Peter 1:10: "Wherefore the rather, brethren, give diligence to make your calling and *election* sure: for if ye do these things, ye shall never fall."

z. Revelation 17:14: "These shall make war with the Lamb, and the Lamb shall overcome them: for he is Lord of lords, and King of kings: and they that are with him are *called,* and *chosen,* and faithful."

3. Election as definite and particular
   a. Deuteronomy 7:6, 1 Kings 3:8, Psalm 105:6, Psalm 132:13, Isaiah 41:8, Isaiah 43:20, Acts 13:17, and other passages of Scripture that speak of God's election of Israel indicate that election is definite. God chose Israel in distinction from all other nations to be His people.
   b. John 15:16: "Ye have not chosen me, but I have chosen *you,* and ordained *you,* that *ye* should go and bring forth fruit."
   c. Romans 8:28–30: "And we know that all things work together for good to *them* that love God, to *them* who are the called according to his purpose. For *whom* he did foreknow, he also did predestinate to be conformed to the image of his Son, that he might be the firstborn among many brethren. Moreover *whom* he did predestinate, *them* he also called; and *whom* he called, *them* he also justified: and *whom* he justified, *them* he also glorified."
   d. Romans 9:11–13: "(For the children being not yet born, neither having done any good or evil, that the purpose of God according to election might stand, not of works, but of him that calleth;) It was said unto her, The elder shall serve the younger. As it is written, *Jacob* have I loved, but Esau have I hated."

In the passage above, the apostle Paul teaches that God has elected the specific, definite person Jacob.

   e. Ephesians 1:4, 5: "According as he hath chosen *us* in him before the foundation of the world, that we should be holy and without blame before him in love: Having predestinated *us* unto the adoption of children by Jesus Christ to himself, according to the good pleasure of his will."

f.   Revelation 13:8: "And all that dwell upon the earth shall worship him [the antichristian beast], whose names are not written in the book of life of the Lamb slain from the foundation of the world."

We are taught in these verses that there are names of definite people written down in the book of life, specific persons, therefore, who are elected by God. The next passage teaches the same truth.

g.   Revelation 17:8: "The beast that thou sawest was, and is not and shall ascend out of the bottomless pit, and go into perdition: and they that dwell on the earth shall wonder, whose names were not written in the book of life from the foundation of the world, when they shall behold the beast that was, and is not, and yet is."

4.   Election as eternal decree
   a.   Ephesians 1:4: "According as he hath chosen us in him *before the foundation of the world,* that we should be holy and without blame before him in love."
   b.   2 Thessalonians 2:13: "But we are bound to give thanks alway to God for you, brethren beloved of the Lord, because God hath *from the beginning* chosen you to salvation through sanctification of the Spirit and belief of the truth."
   c.   2 Timothy 1:9: "Who hath saved us, and called us with an holy calling, not according to our works,

but according to his own purpose and grace, which was given us in Christ Jesus *before the world began.*"

d. Revelation 17:8: "The beast that thou sawest was, and is not; and shall ascend out of the bottomless pit, and go into perdition: and they that dwell on the earth shall wonder, whose names were not written in the book of life *from the foundation of the world,* when they shall behold the beast that was, and is not, and yet is."

5. Election unto salvation
    a. Acts 13:48: "And when the Gentiles heard this, they were glad, and glorified the word of the Lord: and as many as were *ordained to eternal life* believed."
    b. Romans 8:29, 30: "For whom he did foreknow, he also did *predestinate* to be conformed to the image of his Son, that he might be the firstborn among many brethren. Moreover whom he did *predestinate,* them he also called: and whom he called, them he also justified: and whom he justified, them he also glorified."

The "golden chain of salvation" described in Romans 8:29 and 30 begins with *foreknowledge and predestination* and ends with *justification and glorification.*

    c. Ephesians 1:5: *"Having predestinated us unto* the adoption of children by Jesus Christ to himself, according to the good pleasure of his will."
    d. 2 Thessalonians 2:13: "But we are bound to give thanks alway to God for you, brethren beloved of the Lord, because God hath from the beginning

chosen you to *salvation* through sanctification of the Spirit and belief of the truth."

e. 2 Timothy 2:10: "Therefore I endure all things for the elect's sakes, *that they may also obtain the salvation* which is in Christ Jesus *with eternal glory.*"

6. Election as gracious and unconditional

a. Deuteronomy 7:7: "The LORD did not set his love upon you, nor choose you, because ye were more in number than any people; for ye were the fewest of all people."

b. John 1:13: "Which were born, not of blood, nor of the will of the flesh, nor of the will of man, but of God."

c. John 15:16: "Ye have not chosen me, but I have chosen you, and ordained you, that ye should go and bring forth fruit, and that your fruit should remain: that whatsoever ye shall ask of the Father in my name, he may give it you."

d. Romans 9:11: "For the children being not yet born, neither having done any good or evil, that the purpose of God according to *election* might stand, not of works, but of him that calleth."

e. Romans 9:16: "So then it [salvation] is not of him that willeth [man's "free" will], nor of him that runneth [man's works], but of God that sheweth mercy."

f. Romans 11:5: "Even so then at this present time also there is a remnant according to the election of *grace.*"

g. 1 Corinthians 1:27–29: "But God hath chosen the foolish things of the world to confound the wise; and God hath chosen the weak things of the world to confound the things which are mighty; And base things of the world, and things which are despised, hath God chosen, yea, and things which are not, to bring to nought things that are: That no flesh should glory in his presence."

h.   Ephesians 2:8: "For *by grace* are ye saved through faith; and that not of yourselves: it is the gift of God."

i.   2 Timothy 1:9: "Who hath saved us, and called us with an holy calling, not according to our works, but according to his own purpose and *grace,* which was given us in Christ Jesus before the world began."

7. Election as the cause of repentance, faith, and good works

That our election is gracious and unconditional is indicated by those Scripture passages that teach that repentance, faith, and good works are the fruit, not the cause, of our election. It is not that repentance, faith, and good works result in election, but that election is the cause of repentance, faith, and good works.

a.   John 15:16: "Ye have not chosen me, but I have chosen you, and ordained you, *that ye should go and bring forth fruit,* and that your fruit should remain: that whatsoever ye shall ask of the Father in my name, he may give it you."

Jesus clearly teaches that He has chosen and ordained us, not because of the good works ("fruit") that we have produced, but *in order that* we should produce good works. Our good works are not the cause of our election, but the purpose and result of our election.

b. Acts 5:31: "Him [Christ] hath God exalted with his right hand to be a Prince and Saviour, *for to give* repentance to Israel, and forgiveness of sins."

Repentance is not some work that originates in us, a condition that we fulfill, thus making ourselves worthy of God's election of us. On the contrary, repentance is a *gift* of Christ to us. That a man repents is due to the grace of God that works repentance in him.

c. Acts 13:48: "And when the Gentiles heard this [the preaching of the apostle Paul], they were glad, and glorified the word of the Lord: and as many as were ordained to eternal life believed."

This verse indicates that *only* as many as were ordained (elected) to eternal life believed the preaching of God's apostle. It teaches that *all* in his audience who were ordained to eternal life believed. And it teaches that their faith (believing) was the fruit of their having been ordained to eternal life.

d. Ephesians 1:4: "According as he hath chosen us in him before the foundation of the world, *that we should be holy* and without blame before him in love."

We have been chosen so *that* we should be holy and without blame, not *because* we were holy and without blame. Our holiness (good works) is not the basis for our election, but it is the purpose for which we have been elected.

e. Ephesians 2:10: "For we are his workmanship, created in Christ Jesus *unto* good works, which God hath before ordained that we should walk in them."

First, the apostle Paul teaches that we are created in Christ Jesus (saved) *unto* good works. Good works cannot be the cause or basis for our salvation but the goal or purpose for which we are saved. Second, Paul teaches that even the good works that we perform as the result of our salvation "God hath before ordained that we should walk in them." If God has eternally ordained our good work, and if God gives us the strength actually to do good works, how can we ever suppose that our good works are our contribution to salvation, much less the cause of salvation?

>   f.   Acts 18:27: "And when he [Apollos] was disposed to pass into Achaia, the brethren wrote, exhorting the disciples to receive him: who, when he was come, helped them much which had believed *through grace.*"

Like the passage in Ephesians 2:8, this text tells us that faith (believing) is a gift of God. Faith does not originate in man himself, but faith is worked in us by God. To use the language of Acts 18:27, we believe "through grace." Since faith, then, is itself a gracious gift of God, whatever man himself produces cannot be the basis on which his election and salvation depend.

>   g.   2 Timothy 1:9: "Who hath saved us, and called us with an holy calling, *not according to our works, but according to his own purpose and grace,* which was given us in Christ Jesus before the world began."

Paul expressly states that we have been saved and elected not because of any works that God saw in us but according to his will and grace.

> h. Philippians 1:29: "For unto you it is *given* in the behalf of Christ, not only to believe on him, but also to suffer for his sake."

It is *given* to us to believe. Again, Scripture teaches that election and salvation cannot be conditioned on our faith. Faith does not have its source in us who believe; it is a gift of God worked in us.

> i. Philippians 2:12, 13: "Wherefore, my beloved, as ye have always obeyed, not as in my presence only, but now much more in my absence, work out your own salvation with fear and trembling. For it is God which worketh in you both to will and to do of his good pleasure."

Often verse 12 of Philippians 2 is quoted by those who teach that man has the ability to earn his salvation. Emphasis is placed on the exhortation "Work out your own salvation." But that this cannot possibly be the meaning of the words is made plain by the words immediately following: "For it is God *which worketh in you* both to will and to do of his good pleasure." Both our doing of God's good pleasure, as well as our desire to do God's good pleasure, are the fruits of God's work in us.

8. Election in Jesus Christ
   a. Ephesians 1:4: "According as he hath chosen us *in him* before the foundation of the world, that we should be holy and without blame before him in love."

b. Ephesians 1:5: "Having predestinated us unto the adoption of children *by Jesus Christ* to himself, according to the good pleasure of his will."

c. 2 Timothy 1:9: "Who hath saved us, and called us with an holy calling, not according to our works, but according to his own purpose and grace, which was given us *in Christ Jesus* before the world began."

d. Hebrews 5:9: "And being made perfect, *he* [Christ] became the author of eternal salvation unto all them that obey him."

D. Scripture proofs for reprobation

1. Proverbs 16:4: "The LORD hath made all things for himself: yea, even the wicked for the day of evil."

God has made the wicked for the day of evil. They are wicked, willfully wicked. And they forever bear the blame for their wickedness. However, their wickedness does not take away from the fact that they have been made by God *for* the day of evil.

2. John 10:26: "But ye believe not, because ye are not of my sheep, as I said unto you."

Often these words of Jesus to the unbelieving Jews are twisted in a way whereby Jesus is supposed to have said that the unbelieving Jews are not of His sheep (the number of the elect), because they do not believe on Him. That is exactly what Jesus does *not* say in this verse. On the contrary, they do not believe on Him *because they are not of His sheep*. First, they are not of Jesus' sheep. Because they are not, neither do they believe on Him. Implied is that those who *do* believe on Jesus believe on Him because they *are* of His sheep. That they believe on Jesus is itself the evidence that they belong to the number of Jesus' sheep. Because they are of Jesus' sheep, they also believe on Him.

3. Romans 9:11–13: "(For the children being not yet born, neither having done any good or evil, that the purpose of God according to *election* might stand, not of works, but of him that calleth;) It was said unto her, The elder shall serve the younger. As it is written, Jacob have I loved, but Esau have I hated."

4. Romans 9:21–23: "Hath not the potter power over the clay, of the same lump to make one vessel unto honour, *and another unto dishonour*? What if God, willing to shew his wrath, and to make his power known, endured with much long-suffering the vessels of wrath *fitted to destruction:* And that he might make known the riches of his glory on the vessels of mercy, which he had afore prepared unto glory."

5. 1 Thessalonians 5:9: "For God hath not *appointed* us to *wrath,* but to obtain eternal salvation by our Lord Jesus Christ."

That God hath not appointed "us" to wrath definitely implies that there are others who *have* been appointed by God to wrath; in other words, they are reprobated.

6. 1 Peter 2:8: "And a stone of stumbling, and a rock of offence, even to them which stumble at the word, being disobedient: *whereunto also they were appointed.*"

7. Jude 4: "For there are certain men crept in unawares, *who were before of old ordained to this condemnation,* ungodly men, turning the grace of our God into lasciviousness, and denying the only Lord God, and our Lord Jesus Christ."

8. Revelation 13:8: "And all that dwell upon the earth

shall worship him [the antichristian beast], *whose names are not written* in the book of life of the Lamb slain from the foundation of the world."

9. Matthew 11:25, 26: "At that time Jesus answered and said, I thank thee, O Father, Lord of heaven and earth, because thou hast hid these things [of the kingdom] from the wise and prudent, and hast revealed them unto babes. Even so, Father: for so it seemed good in thy sight."

The Lord Jesus thanks—think about that: *thanks*!—His heavenly Father because He has actively hidden the things of the kingdom of heaven from certain men. Jesus indicates that in harmony with the Father's eternal reprobation of some men in time and in history, He hides, hardens, withholds, and blinds certain men, thus *preventing* their salvation.

E. Difficult passages

1. Certain passages of Scripture speak of God's "foreknowledge." Examples are Romans 8:29, "For whom he did *foreknow*, he also did predestinate to be conformed to the image of his Son, that he might be the firstborn among many brethren," and 1 Peter 1:2, "Elect according to the *foreknowledge* of God the Father, through sanctification of the Spirit, unto obedience and sprinkling of the blood of Jesus Christ: Grace unto you, and peace, be multiplied."

The Scripture passages most often used against the doctrine of sovereign unconditional election are those that speak of God's foreknowledge and indicate that foreknowledge precedes election. The argument, then, is that election is not unconditional (without regard for what we are or would be), but is conditioned on God's prior knowledge of what we will be and what we will do. In other words, God chose certain people because He had already foreseen that they would repent and believe. Their foreseen faith is supposedly the condition on which God chose them.

Apart from the fact that this is a denial of God's sovereignty, inasmuch as it makes God's choice dependent on man's choice, it does not at all reflect the biblical idea of foreknowledge. For one thing, foreknowledge in the Scriptures is not just a kind of prophecy of the future, but it is causative. In other words, foreknowledge, as much as election, does not just foretell our believing but actually brings it about (Acts 2:23). For another thing, foreknowledge in the Scriptures is always foreknowledge of a *person,* not merely of a thing or an event. People are foreknown by God. The Scriptures make plain that God's foreknowledge is His love of the elect before time. In the Bible, to "know" is to "love." It is not only to be aware of intellectually, but it is to set one's affection on the one who is known. For this reason the Old Testament customarily refers to the sexual relationship, the highest expression of love between a husband and wife, as their "knowing" each other. Genesis 4:1 is illustrative: "And Adam *knew* Eve his wife; and she conceived, and bare Cain." There are Scriptures that indicate the idea of foreknowledge as God's eternal love for His people. Two examples are Amos 3:2, "You only have I *known* of all the families of the earth: therefore I will punish you for all your iniquities," and Galatians 4:9, "But now, after that ye have *known* God, or rather *are known* of God, how turn ye again to the weak and beggarly elements, whereunto ye desire again to be in bondage?"

Foreknowledge does indeed precede election. In fact, foreknowledge is the deepest reason for election. But foreknowledge in Scripture is not God's knowledge of *our* foreseen faith or good works, but is *God's* eternal love for His people in Christ! The fact that foreknowledge precedes election only means that God's election of us arises out of His love for us. Because in eternity He set His love on us, He chose us to be His elect people in Christ.

2. Deuteronomy 7:6, 7: "For thou art an holy people unto the LORD thy God: the LORD thy God hath chosen thee to be a special people unto himself, above all people that are upon the face of the earth. The LORD did not set his love upon you, nor choose you, because ye were more in number than any people; for ye were the fewest of all people."
3. Deuteronomy 14:2: "For thou art an holy people unto the LORD thy God, and the LORD hath chosen thee to be a peculiar people unto himself, above all the nations that are upon the earth."

Such Old Testament passages that speak of Israel's election are sometimes used to deny that election (and reprobation) are personal and therefore also sovereign and unconditional. Some teach by these verses that God chose only a nation in the Old Testament and that He chose that nation only to receive certain privileges. Similarly it is taught that as far as New Testament people are concerned, God did not choose persons either, but only an indefinite number. Let us understand that if God has chosen certain persons and chosen them to salvation, as the Scriptures so clearly teach, then election is effective and unconditional. But if He has chosen only an indefinite number of persons, or a nation, election is neither effective nor unconditional, for then those who are saved are not saved because of election, but because of their own works or faith.

Especially significant in this connection is Romans 9:10–13, which quotes Old Testament Scripture that obviously speaks of personal election and reprobation. This passage, along with those that speak of "names" being written in the book of life (Luke 10:20, Phil. 4:3, Rev. 13:8, and Rev. 17:8), conclusively show that election is personal, and hence also effective, sovereign, and unconditional.

F. Objections to predestination
1. "Predestination is a denial of God's love."

Often it is objected against the teaching of predestination that it denies a loving God. God is certainly a God of love. In 1 John 4:8 we read, "He that loveth not knoweth not God; for God is love."

What is forgotten, however, is that God loves Himself first of all. He is a jealous God, jealous of His own name, His own righteousness, and His own holiness. Exactly in the love that He has for Himself, God judges, punishes, and damns all who are not in harmony with His own holiness. This shows that God does not *love* everyone. Neither is it true, as is often alleged, that the God of Arminianism is a much more loving God than the God of Calvinism. What sort of love is it when, notwithstanding God's love, some men are not saved but are lost eternally in the sufferings of hell? What would we think of a husband who supposedly loved his wife but did not do good to her, even though he was capable of it? What would we think of parents who supposedly loved their children but abused and injured them, even though it was in their power to do their children good? Strange love, indeed! That is not the nature of the love of God. He does good to all whom He loves, temporally and eternally.

Reprobation serves the purpose of displaying God's justice, as election displays His mercy. In fact, the mercy of God in election is magnified against the dark background of His righteousness in reprobation. This is exactly what Paul teaches in Romans 9:22, 23: "What if God, willing to shew his wrath and to make his power known, endured with much long-suffering the vessels of wrath fitted to destruction: And that he might make known the riches of his glory on the vessels of mercy, which he had afore prepared unto glory?"

2. "Predestination is a denial of God's justice."

Another familiar objection against the doctrine of predestination is that it is not fair or righteous of God to discriminate between men, electing and saving some while rejecting and condemning others.

The apostle Paul faces this objection against predestination in Romans 9:14: "What shall we say then? Is there unrighteousness with God?" The very fact that men raise this objection against us indicates that we are maintaining the same doctrine defended by Paul.

What is our answer to this objection? The same as Paul's: "God forbid!" This objection might have validity if all men alike deserved salvation and God chose and saved only some men. Then there might be room for the accusation that there is unrighteousness in God. But the case is quite different. The reality is that all men are unworthy of God's salvation. All men alike are fallen in Adam, and all men are conceived and born dead in sin. There is no injustice on God's part that out of the entire mass of fallen humanity He should see fit to choose and save some. He is under no obligation to save any. That He should determine to save some is merely a matter of His sovereign mercy: "I will have mercy on whom I will have mercy, and I will have compassion on whom I will have compassion" (Rom. 9:15).

An illustration may help at this point. Suppose that there are ten criminals in a certain kingdom, awaiting execution for their crimes. But for one reason or another, the king of this kingdom chooses to pardon one of the criminals and sets him free. Do the other nine have any right to claim that an injustice has been done to them? Would anyone dare to tell the king that it is unfair that the nine remain in jail and are made to pay for their crimes? Of course not! They deserve to bear the consequences of their sins. The fact that the king chooses to show mercy to one of the criminals in no way obligates him to show mercy to the other nine. Just so, God's mercy in electing and saving some beings is altogether righteous.

3. "Predestination is a denial of man's responsibility."

Yet another often heard objection against the Reformed doctrine of predestination is that it denies man's responsibility and leads to determinism and fatalism. If God has determined whether or not a man is saved and has decided the everlasting destiny of every man, we might as well live as we please. If we have been elected to salvation, we will be saved anyway. If we have been reprobated, there is nothing that we can do to change the will of God. Neither can we really be held responsible for our sins.

This objection, too, is faced by Paul. In Romans 9:19 he writes, "Thou wilt say then unto me, Why doth he [God] yet find fault? For who hath resisted his will?" The very fact that people raise this same objection against us, puts us in good company. It should be no surprise to us that since the apostle faced this objection regarding his teaching of predestination, we must be faced with it, too.

What answer must we give to this objection? The same basic answer as Paul gave: "Nay but, O man, who art thou that repliest against God?" Paul denies the right of puny man to make this objection. He also asks, "Shall the thing formed say to him that formed it, Why hast thou made me thus? Hath not the potter power over the clay, of the same lump to make one vessel unto honour, and another unto dishonour?" (Rom. 9:20, 21).

Two things remain true: God's sovereign predestination *and* man's full responsibility. Paul does not relinquish the doctrine of predestination; neither does he concede to the objection that this teaching denies man's responsibility before God. In a way that transcends our ability fully to explain or comprehend, these two things remain true: God is sovereign, sovereign in determining the everlasting destiny of every man, *and* man remains a responsible, moral, rational creature.

Although the Scriptures are clear about it that God has eternally predestinated all things, they are equally clear in maintaining the full responsibility of the sinner. Several examples bring this out. According to Isaiah 37:21–38, Sennacherib, the king of Assyria, threatened to invade and destroy Judah. Assyria's success in having conquered other nations before this was a result of God's predestination: "Hast thou not heard long ago, how I have done it; and of ancient times, that I have formed it? now have I brought it to pass, that thou [Sennacherib] shouldest be to lay waste defenced cities into ruinous heaps" (Isa. 37:26). But does the fact of God's predestination excuse Sennacherib's behavior? Not at all! God was angry with Sennacherib for his wickedness and punished him for it, even though He had preordained it: "But I know thy abode, and thy going out, and thy coming in, and thy rage against me. Because thy rage against me, and thy tumult, is come up into mine ears, therefore will I put my hook in thy nose, and my bridle in thy lips, and I will turn thee back by the way which thou camest" (Isa. 37:28, 29).

The outstanding example of God's sovereign predestination and man's responsibility is the crucifixion of Christ. In his sermon on Pentecost, Peter declared, "Him [Christ], being delivered by the determinate counsel and foreknowledge of God, ye have taken, and by wicked hands have crucified and slain" (Acts 2:23). Christ's crucifixion took place according to the "determinate counsel and foreknowledge of God." But that did not in the least excuse or minimize the guilt of the "wicked hands" that took Christ and nailed Him to the cross.

4. "Predestination is a denial of missions."

One argument that is often brought against the teaching of predestination is that it precludes missions. The argument is that since God has elected some men, they will be saved, and since he has reprobated others, they will not be saved. What point is there, then, to missions? What this argument overlooks is that not only has God chosen who will be saved, but *how* they will be saved. The means that God has chosen to bring the elect to salvation is the preaching of the gospel. By this preaching, elect sinners are brought to salvation, and the church of Jesus Christ is gathered out of the nations of the world. Election is not a deterrent to missions; it is the reason and purpose for missions. At the same time, the truth of election assures the church of fruit in her mission work. God will use the church's preaching of the gospel so that the elect are saved and gathered. Our assurance is the same as that expressed by the apostle Paul in Acts 13:47: "For so hath the Lord commanded us, saying, I have set thee to be a light of the Gentiles, that thou shouldest be for salvation unto the ends of the earth." The very next verse informs us, "And when the Gentiles heard this, they were glad, and glorified the word of the Lord: and as many as were ordained to eternal life believed" (Acts 13:48).

G. Denials of predestination

Reformed Christians ought to be aware of, and on their guard against, various denials of predestination.

1. Fatalism

The teaching of unconditional election must not be confused with pagan fatalism, which teaches that all things are subject to blind fate and inevitable determinism. According to the fatalist, whatever will be, will be, and the appropriate human response is passive submission to that which is beyond human control.

The Reformed faith repudiates fatalism. Rather than the believer's response to God's sovereign appointment of all things being mere submission to the inevitable, it is gratitude and glory to God who works all things after the counsel of His own will for the ultimate benefit of the believer.

The doctrine of sovereign predestination differs from fatalism, because it teaches the use of the means that God has ordained for the carrying out of His eternal counsel, whereas fatalism promotes passive endurance of that which is inevitable and unavoidable. The Reformed faith points the believer to his calling to make use of the means God has created and graciously provided for His people, all the while resting in God for the benefit of using these means.

The Reformed parent does not take a fatalistic approach towards a wayward child, adopting the view that if it is God's will that his child be restored, God will see to that, and if it is not God's will, there is nothing that he can do to bring about his child's restoration. Instead, he prays earnestly on behalf of his child and brings to his child the warnings of Scripture, availing himself of the means that God has provided for the recovery of those who stray.

2. Free will

Those who teach that natural man—man outside of and apart from the grace of God—is able to choose Jesus Christ and salvation are compelled to deny predestination. Historically this was true of the Pelagians and Arminians. According to those who hold to free will, the decisive choice for salvation is not God's choice but man's choice. All men have the ability to choose, they taught. The unconditional election of Calvinism stands opposed to the teaching of "foreseen faith" by which Arminians say the sinner's act of faith determines God's election, rather than God's election determining man's faith. Election then becomes conditional election. God in eternity simply looks down the corridors of history, sees who will choose Him and who will not, elects those who will, and rejects the rest. Predestination is reduced to mere prescience. God chooses those who will choose Him.

The folly of this teaching ought to be apparent. If salvation depended on man's choice, *no* man would be saved: "There is none righteous, no, not one: There is none that understandeth, there is none that seeketh after God. They are all gone out of the way, they are together become unprofitable; there is none that doeth good, no, not one" (Rom. 3:10–12). The teaching of free will not only denies the total depravity of fallen man, but it is also an assault on God's sovereign predestination. In the clearest possible language Jesus declares in John 15:16, "Ye have not chosen me, but I have chosen you, and ordained you."

3. Common grace

Another serious attack upon the truth of predestination is the teaching of common grace. In large measure, the increasing silence concerning predestination and the denial of it in Reformed and Presbyterian circles today is due to the acceptance of the teaching of common grace. A consistent confession of predestination cannot be made if one also holds to common grace. It is imperative that common grace be repudiated if there is to be a return to the teaching of predestination in these churches.

The teaching of common grace is that God loves all men with a certain non-saving love. God demonstrates this love for all men by giving them all of the good things of this present life. The result is that although God's *saving* love is discriminating (for some only), there is a love of God that embraces all men without distinction.

It is clearly contradictory to say that in eternity God hates and reprobates some men, but in time and history He loves all men. At the very least, this is a denial of God's unchangeableness. At the worst, it leads in the direction of a denial of predestination, particularly reprobation.

This teaching of common grace cannot stand in the light of the Scriptures. In Psalm 5:5 we read, "The foolish shall not stand in thy sight: thou hatest [in the present] all workers of iniquity." In Psalm 11:5 David declares, "The LORD trieth the righteous: but the wicked and him that loveth violence his soul hateth [in the present]." And in Proverbs 3:33 we are told, "The curse of the LORD *is* in the house of the wicked."

4. The free offer of the gospel

The teaching known as the "free offer" or the "well-meant offer" of the gospel is also an implicit denial of sovereign predestination. According to this teaching, God loves and sincerely desires the salvation of all men. Christ has died to make salvation possible for all men. And in the preaching of the gospel, salvation is freely offered to all who hear the gospel. In the end salvation is dependent on whether or not a man accepts the gospel offer.

Certainly, if God has eternally chosen some men unto salvation and rejected and reprobated the rest, it cannot also be true that God sincerely desires to save all men and offers salvation freely to all. This offer is not sincere and leads to the conclusion that God and His gospel are a failure, for who can deny that many to whom the gospel comes reject it, are not saved by it, and perish in their sin and unbelief? Notwithstanding God's so-called love for them and earnest desire to save them, they go lost. It ought not surprise us that in those churches and denominations where there has been acceptance of the teaching of the free offer, there has been an increasing repudiation of sovereign predestination.

All who come under the preaching of the gospel are confronted with their duty before God to repent of their sins and are called (commanded) to faith in Jesus Christ. To tell all men that God loves them, desires to save them, and freely offers them salvation is a misrepresentation of God.

How does this conception of the preaching of the gospel square with God's commission to the prophet Isaiah? Does God send Isaiah out to tell all men that He loves them and wants to save them? On the contrary: "Go, and tell this people, Hear ye indeed, but understand not; and see ye indeed, but perceive not. Make the heart of this people fat, and make their ears heavy, and shut their eyes; lest they see with their eyes, and hear with their ears, and understand with their heart, and convert, and be healed" (Isa. 6:9, 10). Or listen to Christ's words in Matthew 11:25, 26, really a prayer of thanksgiving to God: "I thank thee, O Father, Lord of heaven and earth, because thou hast hid these things [of the kingdom] from the wise and prudent, and hast revealed them unto babes. Even so, Father: for so it seemed good in thy sight." Paul's words in 2 Corinthians 2:14–16 are, "Now thanks be unto God, which always causeth us to triumph in Christ, and maketh manifest the savour of his knowledge by us in every place. For we are unto God a sweet savour of Christ, in them that are saved and in them that perish: To the one we are the savour of death unto death; and to the other the savour of life unto life. And who is sufficient for these things?"

H. Practical importance of predestination

The consistent maintaining of the doctrine of predestination is of the greatest practical importance for the church. It is not true, as its enemies allege, that this doctrine is cold, lifeless, and of no practical value. True doctrine and upright living, both for the individual Christian and for a church, go hand in hand.

1. Predestination and the antithesis

The faithful confession of the doctrine of predestination is vital for the life of the antithesis to which every child of God is called. Denial of predestination, as history shows, inevitably leads to a breakdown of the antithesis.

By the antithesis is meant the separation between the church and the world, and the spiritually separate life the Christian is called to live over against the world. Believers are to be in the world but not of the world. One forceful passage of Scripture that calls believers to the life of the antithesis is 2 Corinthians 6:14–17: "Be ye not unequally yoked together with unbelievers: for what fellowship hath righteousness with unrighteousness? and what communion hath light with darkness? And what concord hath Christ with Belial? Or what part hath he that believeth with an infidel? And what agreement hath the temple of God with idols? for ye are the temple of the living God; as God hath said, I will dwell in them, and walk in them; and I will be their God, and they shall be my people. Wherefore come ye out from among them, and be ye separate, saith the Lord, and touch not the unclean thing; and I will receive you, And will be a Father unto you, and ye shall be my sons and daughters, saith the Lord Almighty."

The denial of predestination always results in an abandoning of the life of the antithesis. This is not difficult to understand. If God loves all men without distinction, then there is a common ground upon which believer and unbeliever can stand. There is room for making a common cause. As some have tried to explain it, Jerusalem and Athens can be married. The outcome is that the church becomes one with the world.

The practical implication of the doctrine of predestination, however, forbids the church making common cause with the world. To use the words of the prophet to King Jehoshaphat, who had sinfully made an alliance with wicked Ahab, "Shouldest thou help the ungodly, and love them that hate the LORD?" (2 Chron. 19:2)

2. Predestination and the preaching of the gospel

The truth of election provides the church with the motivation to preach the gospel in all the world to every creature. The enemies of election charge that predestination negates the necessity and importance of the preaching of the gospel. If the elect have been eternally predestinated by God to salvation, it is alleged, there is no need for them to hear the gospel. They will be saved anyway. Sometimes it is even said that those who hold to the doctrine of predestination should preach *only* to the elect! This can result in a slanderous misrepresentation; even in its mildest form this error is a serious misunderstanding of the truth of election. Election in no way rules out *the means* by which God has ordained that the elect shall be brought to salvation, namely, *the preaching of the gospel*. The same God who has ordained the elect unto salvation has also ordained the means by which they shall be brought to salvation and to the assurance of their election. The warning of the Canons of Dordt, III/IV, Article 17, is to the point: "Be it far from either instructors or instructed to presume to tempt God in the church by separating what he of his good pleasure hath most intimately joined together."

God has scattered the elect in every nation, tongue, and

tribe under heaven. The means He has ordained for their faith and salvation is the preaching of the gospel. Thus, the church has the divine mandate to go into all the world and preach the gospel.

Nor must it be supposed that the preaching of the gospel serves no purpose with the reprobate who come under the preaching. On the contrary, they are confronted squarely with their duty and warned against their unbelief. Their rejection of the gospel serves to aggravate their guilt and leaves them without excuse before God.

At the same time, the truth of election gives the church confidence in preaching the gospel, whether in the established congregation to the sons and daughters born in the church, or to the unsaved in missions. The elect *will* hear that preaching. By that preaching they *will* be brought to repentance and faith. The people of God *will* be saved. The church has that assurance as she preaches.

3. Predestination and humility

The truth of election also gives reason for profound humility on the part of believers. Is there anything so needed in the church today as humility? The believer is humbled by the truth that his salvation is not due to anything he is or anything he has done, but it is due alone to the predestinating grace of God. The believer is humbled by the realization that he was not better than those whom God did not choose, that indeed he himself was involved in a common ruin. Salvation does not have its cause in us, but in the will and good pleasure of God alone. "Where is boasting then? It is excluded" (Rom. 3:27). If God's choice of us depended on our choice of Him, if our assumed "free will," rather than the will of God, was decisive for salvation, we would have reason to boast in ourselves. The truth of sovereign, gracious election takes this possibility away. It is a truth that can but lead to humility in the life of one who sincerely confesses it.

4. Predestination and assurance

The truth of predestination is of the greatest practical value in relation to the assurance of the believer. Often the question is asked, "How may I know that I am an elect child of God?" At times in his life, the believer may struggle with doubts concerning his salvation. The way to the assurance of election and salvation is obviously not flying up to heaven to peer into God's book of life to see if one's name is written down there. Neither is the way to assurance some special revelation or arresting experience from God. But the way is the observation of the fruits of election in one's life. Do you believe on God's Son, Jesus Christ? Are you sorry for your sins? Do you delight in the Word and worship of God? Do you strive to keep God's commandments? All these, and many more besides, are the fruits of election. That you observe these fruits in your life means—can only mean—that you are an elect child of God. Believe that! Be assured of it! Live in that joy and assurance with thankfulness to God!

5. Predestination and God's glory

Not only does the truth of predestination remove every cause for glorying in self; it also ascribes the glory for salvation to God. God has chosen us to salvation. God has delivered us from the common misery in which we had involved ourselves. God has determined everything needful for our salvation: the sending of His own Son, the preaching of the gospel, the work in us of the Holy Spirit. It is all of Him and nothing of us. To Him and to Him alone must be the glory: "For of him, and through him, and to him, are all things: to whom be glory for ever" (Rom. 11:36).

I. Relation of unconditional election to the other four points

The truth of total depravity necessitates unconditional election. By nature man is dead in sin, capable neither of saving himself nor desiring to be saved. He is in no position to accomplish or to cooperate in his salvation. If man is really totally depraved—we must do justice to this truth—the cause of salvation must be in God, as the truth of election teaches that it is.

The truth of election also limits the scope of the death of Christ. Here there is perfect agreement between the will of the Father and the work of the Son. If some only are chosen to salvation and Christ has died only for those whom God has chosen, Christ's death must be limited to some men only. His redemption is a particular redemption. He has not died, neither did He intend to die, for all men but for some only, for the elect.

If God has chosen us to salvation, so that the almighty will of God Himself rather than the fickle will of man stands behind our election, we may be certain that we *shall* be saved. No power of the devil, of the wicked world, or of ourselves is able to withstand the power of almighty God. Hence, the truth of sovereign election implies the irresistibility of grace.

The doctrine of election also gives us confidence of our perseverance in faith and salvation. If my salvation depended on my will, my choice, my decision, then I could never have the assurance of perseverance. Always I would be in doubt whether the same will that brought me into salvation might also take me out of salvation. However, since the cause of my salvation does not rest in my own will but in the almighty will of an unchangeable God, I can rest assured that I will persevere to the end. We may be confident that the good work He has begun in us shall by the power of His grace be fully accomplished (Phil. 1:6).

CHAPTER IV

Limited Atonement

The doctrine of limited atonement is the third of the Five Points of Calvinism and is represented by the letter *L* in the word *TULIP,* the word we use to help us remember the five points and their order.

This doctrine has been given other names. It is sometimes spoken of as the doctrine of "particular atonement," "particular redemption," or "definite redemption," for reasons that we will see later.

It is also, so it seems, the most difficult of the Five Points to receive and believe as the teaching of the Scriptures, though the Bible does, certainly, teach this doctrine. For this reason, limited atonement is often rejected by those who are Calvinistic in their other teachings, so that there are some who claim to be "Four-point Calvinists," accepting the other four points and rejecting this one. This is really an impossibility, since all five of these doctrines "hang together" and are impossible to separate from one another. Nevertheless, the fact that some do attempt to be Four-point Calvinists indicates the difficulty of this doctrine.

It is regrettable that the doctrine is attacked and denied, since it concerns the work of Christ on the cross and the benefits of that work for God's people. What ought to be a source of fellowship, of unity, and of mutual faith in the death and redemptive work of Jesus Christ has become instead a matter of division and even strife among those who believe differently. Let it be clear that it is not our intent in treating this doctrine to further that strife or cause division but to show as clearly as possible the teaching of Scripture in the hope that this may bring unity and fellowship in the truth.

A. The doctrine
1. Atonement

Whenever we speak of the atonement, we are using one of the words that the Bible itself uses to describe the benefits of Christ's death. The word, at least in the Old Testament, means "a covering" and reminds us that Christ's death provides a covering for our sins before God. The English word refers to the fact that through the death of Christ, God's people are "reconciled" or "at one" with Him. The death of Christ, in other words, is "at-one-ment." The Bible, of course, uses many other words to describe the death of Christ and its benefits, words such as "ransom," "reconciliation," "propitiation," "satisfaction," and "redemption." All of these words differ somewhat in meaning, but they have this in common: they indicate that Christ's death is our salvation.

It really does not matter whether we use the word "atonement" or one of these other words. The disagreement does not revolve around any of these words and their meanings, but around the word "limited" when it is added to the word "atonement" or to any other of these words. No one would dispute that Christ's death is atonement, ransom, reconciliation, propitiation, or redemption. Those who believe in limited atonement believe also in limited redemption, limited satisfaction, limited propitiation, and all the rest, while the opponents of this doctrine would reject the word "limited" when used in connection with any of the words that describe the saving power of the death of Christ and would teach a *universal* atonement or redemption or satisfaction. It is nevertheless very important to see that all of the words used to describe the death of Christ have this in common: they emphasize that Christ's death *actually saves*. This is at the heart of the continuing dispute over this doctrine.

2. Limited

When we add the word "limited," we are answering the question, "For whom did Christ die?" Did He die for every single person who ever has lived and ever will live, or did He die only for some people?

The doctrine of limited atonement teaches that Christ died only for some persons, a "limited" number of persons. Those who teach this doctrine would agree that the "limitation" on the atonement is election. In other words, Christ died only for the elect, and it is only the elect who benefit from Christ's death.

Some clarification is needed here, for most of those who believe in an unlimited or universal atonement do not believe that everyone benefits from the death of Christ in the sense that everyone is finally saved. They believe that Christ died for every person and that salvation is made available to everyone through the death of Christ, but that some only (those who believe) benefit fully from Christ's death.

On the other hand, those who believe in limited atonement do not teach that the *power* and *value* of Christ's death are in any way limited. The only thing limited is the *number* of those for whom Christ died, and the limitation is not due to any defect in the work or death of Christ, but to God's sovereign decree to save some and not others. For this reason, many who teach and believe in limited atonement prefer to speak of "particular atonement" rather than "limited atonement," since the word "particular" much more accurately describes what they believe, that is, that Christ died only for particular persons and not for all people. The word "particular" also leaves no doubt about what exactly is limited.

3. Possibility or guarantee?

There is another aspect of this doctrine, however, which is not immediately apparent and which is sometimes missed in a discussion of it. That is the question as to what Christ actually did by His death on the cross. The doctrine of limited atonement teaches that Christ by His death *actually saves* those for whom He died and does not just make salvation a *possibility.* In other words, His death *is* reconciliation with God, satisfaction for sin, redemption, atonement, and all the rest, and it *guarantees* eternal life to all those for whom He died. This would seem self-evident, but it is exactly this point that must be compromised in order to teach that Christ died for all men without actually and completely saving all of them.

If Christ died for all without exception, and some still perish, then Christ's death only makes salvation *possible,* but it does not *actually* save anyone. Something else is needed for salvation above and beyond the death of Christ. This something else is usually thought to be man's choice or decision. That, however, means salvation is not by Christ *alone* and by His blood *alone.*

In summary, therefore, the doctrine of limited atonement teaches four things:

    a.   Christ's death is atonement for sin.
    b.   Because it is atonement, all those for whom He died are really and completely saved and go to heaven.
    c.   Christ died only for particular persons and not for every single person who has lived or will live.

    d. Those particular persons for whom Christ died are the elect, that is, those whom God chose in eternity to be His people.

B. Scripture proofs
  1. Primary references
    a. Matthew 1:21: "And she shall bring forth a son, and thou shalt call his name JESUS: for he *shall* save *his people* from their sins."

Notice the emphasis on "his people." They are the ones Jesus saves and no others. Whoever they may be (and the Scriptures teach us in other places that they are the elect), they are a limited and particular number of persons. But notice also the emphasis on the fact that He *does* save them. He does not merely make salvation *available* but saves them from their sins *entirely*. Most important of all is the fact that these are the reasons why He is called JESUS. To deny either of these things is to deny His name and the meaning of His name.

    b. Isaiah 53:11: "He shall see of the travail of his soul, and shall be satisfied: by his knowledge shall my righteous servant justify many; for he shall bear their iniquities."
    c. Matthew 20:28: "Even as the Son of man came not to be ministered unto, but to minister, and to give his life a ransom for many."
    d. Matthew 26:28: "For this is my blood of the new testament, which is shed for many for the remission of sins."
    e. Hebrews 9:28: "So Christ was once offered to bear the sins of many; and unto them that look for him shall he appear the second time without sin unto salvation."

All four of these texts show that Christ gave His life for a select and limited number of persons and not for every single person. This is not to deny that there are also passages that speak of "all" or of the "world"; but if the Bible is indeed the infallible Word of God, the two types of passages cannot contradict each other. Either it must be shown that "many" somehow means "every single person," or it must be shown that "all" and "world" do not necessarily refer to every single person living or who has lived.

Scripture also reminds us here that the gift of Christ's life was real and full satisfaction and justification for this "many." His death was a ransom that actually purchased them out of the slavery of sin and death and that truly remits their sins, that is, sends their sins away.

> f. John 6:37–39: "All that the Father giveth me shall come to me; and him that cometh to me I will in no wise cast out. For I came down from heaven, not to do mine own will, but the will of him that sent me. And this is the Father's will which hath sent me, that of all which he hath given me I should lose nothing, but should raise it up again at the last day."

Christ loses none of those for whom He does His work. It is not as though Christ comes for all and yet loses many who slip away or do not believe. If He had lost even one of those for whom He came, He would not have done the Father's will, and His work would not even have been approved of God. Thus we see, too, that it was not even God's will that Christ should die for or make salvation possible for all men. The ones for whom He comes and does His work are those given Him by the Father, the elect, those chosen by God before the foundations of the world.

The passage is also valuable because it gives clear guidance as to how the word "all" is used in the Scriptures. We may not forget that it is used here and further defined as "all whom the Father giveth me." The "all" for whom Christ died, as this passage shows so clearly, never includes anyone but "all" the elect.

g.   John 10:14, 15: "I am the good shepherd, and know my sheep, and am known of mine. As the Father knoweth me, even so know I the Father: and I lay down my life for the sheep."

Jesus not only teaches limited atonement by emphasizing that it is His *sheep* for whom He died, but He also plainly teaches what we have previously called "particular" atonement. He tells us that He knows His sheep in the same way that the Father knows Him and He knows the Father, that is, personally and by name. If this is true, if He laid down His life for those whom He knows personally, then He cannot have died merely so that anyone and everyone might have a chance at salvation.

h.   John 10:26–28: "But ye believe not, because ye are not of my sheep, as I said unto you. My sheep hear my voice, and I know them, and they follow me: And I give unto them eternal life; and they shall never perish, neither shall any man pluck them out of my hand."

That Christ actually saves His sheep by His death, saves them all the way to heavenly glory, infallibly and completely, is taught in the verses quoted. These verses show, too, that it is not our faith that determines whether we will profit from Christ's death, but the will of God. In other words, as Jesus tells the unbelieving Jews, they are not excluded from the sheep because they do not believe; but because they are not of His sheep, they do not believe. Because He did not die for them, they do not receive the gift of faith that He purchases for us with His own blood, nor any of the other blessings of salvation.

> i.   Acts 20:28: "Take heed therefore unto yourselves, and to all the flock, over the which the Holy Ghost hath made you overseers, to feed the church of God, which he hath purchased with his own blood."

Paul also identifies those for whom the blood of Christ was shed as a limited and particular number of persons, the church. And when we remember that in Scripture God's church, as contrasted with the world, is a group drawn and called *out of the world,* this makes the text even more emphatic.

> j.   Isaiah 53:8: "He was taken from prison and from judgment: and who shall declare his generation? for he was cut off out of the land of the living: for the transgression of *my people* was he stricken."
>
> k.   Luke 1:68: "Blessed be the Lord God of Israel; for he hath visited and redeemed *his people.*"

Here are two more passages that define those for whom Christ gave His life as "His people" or even "My people" (God Himself speaking). Surely the wicked and unbelieving cannot be called that!

> l.   Titus 2:13, 14: "Looking for that blessed hope, and the glorious appearing of the great God and our

Saviour Jesus Christ; Who gave himself for *us,* that he might redeem *us* from all iniquity, and purify unto himself a peculiar people, zealous of all good works."

m. Galatians 3:13: "Christ hath redeemed *us* from the curse of the law, being made a curse for *us:* for it is written, Cursed is every one that hangeth on a tree."

In these last two verses, Scripture defines those who benefit from Christ's redemptive work as "us," and the word used is, by its very nature, exclusive rather than inclusive. Titus 2:13, 14 is especially significant, not only because it speaks of Christ giving Himself for us, but also because it shows that those for whom He gave Himself are surely and completely saved—redeemed, purified, and zealous of good works.

2. Passages showing that Christ fully saves those for whom He died

Many of the passages quoted above demonstrate clearly that Christ's death does not just make salvation a possibility, so that it depends on our accepting it to become a saving death, but that it *is* salvation and the *guarantee* of eternal life for all those for whom He died. Since this is the real issue in the debate over limited atonement, we add the following verses to those previously quoted.

a. Luke 19:10: "For the Son of man is come to seek and *to save* that which was lost."

Notice that Christ comes *to save* the lost, not just to make it possible for them to be saved, the lost being those who *know* themselves lost like Zacchaeus. What is especially important about this verse, though, is that it is an explanation of the previous verse, as indicated by the word "For." In that previous verse Jesus says, "This day is salvation come to this house." Salvation came, therefore, to the house of Zacchaeus not because he believed, but *because* the Son of man comes *to save.*

> b. Romans 5:8–10: "But God commended his love toward us, in that, while we were yet sinners, Christ died for us. Much more then, being now justified by his blood, we *shall be saved* from wrath through him. For if, when we were enemies, we were reconciled to God by the death of his Son, much more, being reconciled, we *shall be saved* by his life."

The point cannot be made any more clearly. We *are reconciled* to God by the death of Christ. That means that there is nothing anymore that is between God and us, nor *can* anything come between us, for having been reconciled, we *shall* be saved. This is, of course, more a reference to the final glory of God's people than to their first receiving it, but that in no wise lessens the emphasis of the text. If anything, it makes the text even stronger, for the death of Christ guarantees not only the beginning of salvation but eternal life itself and heavenly glory. What is more, the passage is repeating and reemphasizing that point, for it has already stated that we *are* justified by His blood (and therefore have peace with God, verse 5:1); and being justified, we shall surely be saved from wrath. The line of thought, therefore, is this: Christ's death justifies; because it justifies, it surely saves us from God's wrath; therefore, there is no possibility of condemnation for anyone for whom Christ died but only assurance of life everlasting.

    c.   1 Peter 2:24: "Who his own self bare our sins in his own body on the tree, that we, being dead to sins, should live unto righteousness: by whose stripes ye *were healed.*"

Not only Christ's death but all His suffering (his "stripes") has actual saving power. It is to us the death of sin and the beginning of a new life of righteousness, as well as our healing. It is not merely the possibility of healing, but by it we *were* (literally, "have been") healed.

C. Difficult passages

Many passages are used to teach that Christ died for all men without exception simply because they have in them the words "all" or "world." Rather than deal with each passage separately, we will group them as to the word they use and deal with them by choosing a few representative examples to show how they must all be interpreted in the light of the rest of Scripture. Generally speaking, it may be said that these passages do not intend to show that Christ died for all men *without exception,* but that He died for all men *without distinction,* that is, making no difference between Jew or Gentile, great or small, rich or poor, slave or master.

1. "All" passages

First are those passages that use the word "all" in connection with Christ's death. The best known are Romans 5:18; 2 Corinthians 5:14, 15; 1 Timothy 2:4–6; Titus 2:11; and 2 Peter 3:9.

    In these passages the word "all" must be qualified by the context and usually means "all the elect" or "all God's people." But in every case the Scriptures themselves provide the qualifier. Nor is this unusual. We speak that way so often in our everyday talk that we hardly realize it, simply using the word "all" when we are actually referring to a rather limited number of people; but we do not add the qualifier, because in the context of what we have been saying, it is already obvious. We say, "All are here" and mean "all who were invited," or "all the family," not "all men without exception."

Thus, in 1 Corinthians 15:22 "all" means "all who are in Christ." This is the parallel to "all who are in Adam" and who die in Adam. In fact, the text cannot mean anything else, or it teaches that every single person will ultimately be saved, something plainly contradictory to the rest of the Scriptures. Hardly anyone dares believe that all without exception shall be made alive.

So also in 1 Timothy 2:4–6 "all" plainly means "all *kinds* of men," not just ordinary people, but also rulers and governors and those who are in authority. That is the context of the statement that Christ is the Mediator of "all" and that God wills "all" to be saved. Paul begins with that idea in verse 1 where he admonishes the church to pray for *all kinds* of persons, especially for rulers, something they had been neglecting. He is not telling them to pray for every single person in the world, a manifest impossibility. And so in the following verses he does not introduce a new thought but simply follows up the admonition with various reasons: that God has willed the salvation of *all kinds* of persons and that Christ is the Mediator of *all kinds* of persons.

Other passages that use the word "all" in this same way to mean "all kinds" or "all manner" are Matthew 4:23, Matthew 5:11, Matthew 10:1, Luke 11:42, Acts 10:12, Romans 7:8, 1 Peter 1:15, and Revelation 21:19. In many of these verses, in fact, that is the only thing the word "all" *can* mean. Even though they do not refer directly to the death of

Christ, they nevertheless do establish the way the word "all" can be and is used in the Scriptures.

Similar is Titus 2:11. If this passage teaches that the grace of God in the cross is for all men without exception, it not only contradicts some of the passages we have already cited, but it contradicts the rest of Titus 2 as well, particularly verses 13 and 14, which say that that grace and salvation were revealed for *us,* by which Paul refers to the church.

Likewise 2 Peter 3:9 cannot mean that God is waiting for every single person to come to Christ and to repentance. If that were true, Christ would never come, for that is what is being "delayed." Christ cannot and will not come until "all" have come to repentance. If He must wait for all men without exception, He will wait forever. But He waits for "us," that is, for a preordained group, and when their number is complete, He comes as He has promised. The verse itself defines "all" as "all of us" and tells us that it is "all of us" to whom God is longsuffering and for whom He is waiting.

So it is with all the passages that use this language.

2. "World" passages

Other passages use the word "world" to identify those for whom Christ died. The most often quoted passages using this language are John 1:29, John 3:16, John 4:42, and 1 John 2:2. Those less often quoted are 2 Corinthians 5:19 and 1 John 4:14. These passages, too, must be understood in light of the rest of the Word of God. The key is John 17:9, which shows that there are two worlds, one for which Christ does not even pray, much less die (for if He could die for it, surely He could and would pray for it), and another world for which He both prays and dies: "I pray for them: I pray not for the world, but for them which thou hast given me; for they are thine." Most of the passages must be interpreted with this in mind.

In a few of these passages, the reference of the word "world" is not so much to the world of the elect in distinction from the world of the wicked reprobate, but to the world of the Gentiles in distinction from the world of Jews. But even then, there are two worlds, though both are redeemed by the blood of Christ. The most notable is 1 John 2:2.

There is a reason why the Bible uses these words when speaking of the death of Christ. It does not use them merely to make things difficult or to cause confusion, but to teach a very important truth. That truth is this: that God, in saving His people, does save the *world*. His work of salvation is not some kind of salvage work by which He manages to rescue a few here and there, but it is the salvation of the world that He originally created, though because of sin it involves the cutting off and destruction of many persons. In other words, in the same way that God saves His "vine" in Isaiah 5 and saves it by cutting off many of the branches, so God saves His world. It is important that we see salvation from this perspective, since it shows us that God is not frustrated by the coming of sin so that the best He can do is to pick up the stray pieces of the wreckage of His plans, but that He in perfect wisdom accomplishes His original purpose and saves His world.[1]

3. 1 Timothy 4:10 and 2 Peter 2:1

A few other verses need to be dealt with, notably 1 Timothy 4:10 and 2 Peter 2:1. The first would seem to teach that God, in addition to being the Savior of His people, is also in some sense the Savior of all men. 2 Peter 2:1 would seem to teach that the Lord in some sense of the word also "purchased" those who deny Him and are finally destroyed.

As far as 1 Timothy 4:10 is concerned, it cannot mean that God is the Savior of all men in the usual sense of the word, because otherwise the passage would contradict the rest of the

Scriptures and teach universalism, the teaching that no one will be damned. Notice that the verse does not just say that God sent His Son for all, but that He is the Savior of all. The explanation we prefer, though Calvin gives an alternative, has to do with the use of the word "specially." The word "all" seems to indicate that "all men" is a larger and less exclusive group than "those that believe." In fact, they are the same group. The idea of the verse is therefore this: "The Saviour of all men, *that is,* of those that believe."

Three other verses in the New Testament use the same word translated "specially" and "chiefly" in that way. In Acts 25:26 "you" and "king Agrippa" are the same person, so that the verse can be read, "before you, *that is,* before thee, O king Agrippa." In 1 Timothy 5:8 "his own" and "those of his own house" are also the same group, and the word "specially" again has the idea of "that is." Thus, everyone is command-ed to care for "his own, *that is,* for those of his own house." Finally, in 2 Peter 2:9, 10 the "unjust" and "them that walk after the flesh" are the same group of people, and the word translated "chiefly" again has the idea of "that is." God re-serves "the unjust unto the day of judgment to be punished, *that is,* them that walk after the flesh."

Insofar as the word has any other meaning, it indicates that the group referred to in each case has a *special* name, a name that reinforces what each passage says about them. In Acts 25:26 "you" is "king Agrippa." In 1 Timothy 5:8 "his own" are "those of his own house," reinforcing the command to care for them. And in 2 Peter 2:9, 10, the "unjust" are "those that walk after the flesh," emphasizing the reason that they are reserved unto judgment.

So in 1 Timothy 4:10 "all men" are especially "those that believe," and the text is explaining by the second name why God is their Savior. Thus, the verse, instead of suggesting that God in some sense is Savior of all men without exception, actually shows that "all men" is the equivalent of "those that believe," a limited number of persons.

With respect to 2 Peter 2:1, it must be remembered, first of all, that the passage cannot mean that these people were actually purchased by Christ with His own blood. If that were the case, they would belong to Christ and belong to Him forever, for as Jesus says in John 10:28, "I give unto them eternal life; and they shall never perish, neither shall any man pluck them out of my hand." Keeping that in mind, there are several possible ways to interpret 2 Peter 2:1. The first would simply make the words "the Lord that bought them" a reference to the truth of blood atonement as taught by and believed in the church, leaving the reference of the pronoun "them" general and *not* a reference to these false prophets. These false prophets deny the confession of the church, "the Lord bought us." The other interpretation is very similar and would make the word "them" refer back to "people" instead of making it refer to the false teachers. Those who are bought by the blood of Christ, then, are the people of God in the past and also in the present (those to whom Peter is writing).

In conclusion, let the point made above be stressed again: if the passages that seem to teach Christ died for all men without exception are carefully examined and then interpreted as a reference to every single person without exception, one will find that they teach far more than those who believe in universal atonement want them to teach. Then they teach not just that Christ died for all men without exception, but that all of them are actually saved and go to heaven.

D. Objections

1. "Limited atonement devalues Christ's death."

An objection often heard against the doctrine of limited or particular atonement is that it limits the *value* of Christ's sacrifice by teaching that Christ died only for some and not for all. Actually, this is the very opposite of the truth. It is not limited atonement that denies the value of Christ's death, but the teaching that Christ in some sense died for all.

The point is that if Christ died for all, and all are not in fact really and completely saved by His death, then Christ's death really did not do very much for them. It did not even determine whether or not they would perish or be saved. Christ's sacrifice, in that case, is neither very powerful nor very valuable.

But if all those for whom Christ died, even if they are not all men everywhere, are truly and fully saved by His sacrifice, then His blood is indeed beyond price because of its saving power. Only the doctrine of limited atonement, which teaches that Christ's death is the *full* salvation of all those for whom He died, is able, therefore, to show the infinite *value* of our Savior's sacrifice.

2. "Limited atonement inhibits missions."

Some think that sinners will not be drawn to Christ under the preaching of the gospel unless they can be told, "Christ died for you." They can be told that, of course, only if Christ did die for everyone.

Really the opposite is true. It is not the doctrine of limited atonement that inhibits missions and gospel preaching, but the doctrine of universal atonement. We know from personal experience that to tell sinners, "Christ died for you, because He died for all" is dangerous. The response of most in that case is, "If God loves me, and Christ died for me, then all is well. Why should I worry?"

There is nothing, therefore, that has produced more carnal security, both among both professing believers and among unbelievers than the teaching that Christ died for all without exception. For this reason alone, it must be rejected.

3. "Limited atonement destroys assurance."

Some suggest that only the teaching that Christ died for all can produce assurance. Only then can I believe that Christ died for *me*.

This simply is not true. There is no real assurance to be gained from the teaching that Christ died for all, and that some still perish. Such teaching will leave me always questioning whether I will be, after all, among those who perish, even though Christ died for me.

E. Denials of limited atonement

As with the other four points of Calvinism, the doctrine of limited atonement has also been denied in various ways throughout the history of the church.

1. Universalism

This teaching says that all men actually are saved by the blood of Christ and makes its appeal to those passages that speak of "all men" or of "the world." There is a difference between this teaching and that of Arminianism. Arminianism says Christ died for all, but all do not actually benefit from Christ's death. Not all for whom He died go to heaven. Universalism says that no one goes to hell and that the blood of Christ avails for all without exception.

Any cursory study of the Scriptures' teaching on judgment and hell will show that this teaching is false. Nevertheless, as obviously contrary as it is to the Bible, it is in some ways more consistent and more correct than the idea that Christ died only to make salvation possible. At least universalism does not deny the power of the blood of Christ to save. Christ died for all, they say, and therefore all will certainly be saved.

In fact, if we are to maintain that Christ's death has saving power, universalism is the only possible argument against Calvinism.

2. Roman Catholicism

The Roman Catholic Church denies the doctrine of limited atonement not so much by denying that Christ died only for His people, but by denying that His blood is the only thing that cleanses away sin and by denying that He removed the sins of His people once for all. Thus, such things as good works, penance, and purgatory are required in addition to the blood of Christ to purge away sin. Likewise, the merits and prayers of the saints and of Mary are of as much value as Christ's work in forgiving sins. Especially the Roman Catholic mass, which supposedly is a non-bloody reenactment of the death of Christ, is a clear denial of the once-for-all-time value of Christ's death.

However, the Roman Catholic Church also denies the limited character of the atonement by teaching that there are more for whom the blood of Christ avails than those who finally go to heaven. For example, according to Roman Catholic teaching, the blood of Christ through the sacrament of baptism actually washes away original sin, including the original sin of some who do not continue in the way of salvation.

3. Arminianism

Arminianism, against which the original Five Points of Calvinism (the Canons of Dordt) were written, taught and still teaches today that Christ died for all men, though all are not actually saved and do not all go to heaven. They explain this by teaching that Christ through His death made salvation *available* to all, and that whether or not a person actually profits from the death of Christ depends on his believing and accepting what Christ has done.

This, however, makes our salvation depend more on our own choice or decision than on the death of Christ, and denies the power of Christ's blood. As the Canons of Dordt point out, this means that Christ might have died without anyone actually profiting from His death (Canons II, Rejection of Errors, 3), something that does not speak well of the wisdom of God in sending Christ or of the value of Christ's death. In this way it is a denial of the power and value of His death, though this is the charge often leveled against Calvinism by those who believe that Christ died for all men.

4. The free offer of the gospel

This pestiferous teaching has crept into Reformed theology in recent years and is an "enemy in the camp" in that it also constitutes a denial of limited atonement. This error says that God in the gospel makes a sincere and well-meaning offer of salvation to every person who hears the gospel, expressing His desire that all be saved.

If this is true, God is a liar in the preaching of the gospel, for He says what is not true according to the doctrine of limited atonement. His will as revealed in the cross is not that He desires the salvation of all men, but of some only, that is, of His elect. Nor did He send His Son for all men, but for the elect. How, then, can God sincerely say in the gospel that He wants all men to be saved without contradicting Himself and making Himself a liar?

Moreover, it is self-evident that if God really does express in the gospel a desire that all men be saved, the only possible basis for this can be that in some sense of the word, He also sent Christ to die for all men. But that is not limited atonement.

Such teaching is explicitly rejected in the Canons of Dordt

as part of the erroneous teaching of the Arminians (Canons III, IV, Rejection of Errors, 5). It also does serious damage to the cause of Calvinism, for it is the teaching of many who claim to believe in limited atonement, but who actually contradict limited atonement at this very point.

5. Modernism

This is not the name of any particular sect or denomination but a reference to the teaching, so common today, that the death of Christ is not even atonement or redemption, but merely an example of a man who was willing to die for his principles—an example that we must follow. This teaching would make the death of Christ an example for all, at least for all who care to give heed to it, but it is clear that by denying the redemptive character of the blood of Christ, those who so teach are outside the pale of Christianity, for the death and atoning sacrifice of Christ are the very principles on which Christianity is founded.

The reason for mentioning this, however, is that in essence the teaching of modernism is not that much different from the teaching of Arminianism, which also denies the power and efficacy of the blood of Christ. In fact, at the time of the Synod of Dordt, the Arminians were teaching various theories of the atonement that made the atonement merely an example of God's love or of His justice and that explicitly denied that the atonement was anything more than an example.

6. Sufficiency and efficiency

Some teach that while the death of Christ was savingly powerful only for the elect, it was nevertheless sufficiently valuable to have paid for the sins of all mankind. This in itself is rather abstract and perhaps not overly objectionable, though the Scriptures certainly do not make such a distinction. The

Bible insists that the atonement is both powerful and valuable only for the elect. However, this distinction is usually carried a step further, and it is taught that the death of Christ was not only valuable enough to pay for the sins of all, but that God actually intended it to do that. The only reason it does not, according to this view, is man's stubbornness in not believing and accepting the work of Christ. This teaching is but thinly disguised Arminianism and a denial of the particular and limited character of the atonement.

7. The love of God for all men

Obviously, the whole discussion of the extent of the atonement is inseparably connected with a discussion of God's love and God's intention. The teaching that Christ died for all without exception follows from the belief that God loves all and wants all to be saved. There is, then, a very close connection between the doctrines of limited atonement and unconditional election. The Calvinist does not only believe that Christ died for a limited number because that is the teaching of the Bible, but also because he believes that the Bible teaches sovereign, unconditional election, that is, that God eternally loves and intends to save only some, but not all.

Nevertheless, it should be pointed out that if God is God, and if Christ is His beloved Son, God's intention and love cannot contradict what Christ did by His death. Christ's work cannot be anything but a fulfilling of God's love and intention.

F. Practical importance

The doctrine of limited atonement is not a mere abstraction but part of the truth that rules our lives, makes us holy and obedient, and gives us our comfort. With that in mind, let us look at some of the practical implications of the doctrine.

1. Limited atonement and preaching

Whether or not one believes in limited atonement makes a tremendous difference in the way one preaches the gospel. If the cross is indeed the power of God unto salvation, as the Scriptures tell us it is, then the preaching will be the *proclamation* of the cross and of Christ's death on the cross. Then the power by which sinners believe will be the power of God speaking to them through that proclamation and by His Spirit working in their hearts.

If, however, the power of the cross depends on man's accepting or believing it, the preaching will degenerate into a kind of "sales pitch," as in many cases it does. One need only witness the various revival meetings that are so popular, the advent of the altar call, and the begging and pleading with sinners that is introduced into the worship of the church and into evangelism. In them one sees what the preaching becomes when the truth of limited, efficacious atonement is denied. It becomes, in the words of another writer, a "hawking" of Jesus Christ and of the cross on the order of, and very much like, what goes on at a carnival.

This is not to deny that there must also go forth as part of the preaching of the cross the call to repent and believe, but if one truly believes in limited atonement, that will indeed be a *call* in the sense of a command and not a thinly disguised *offer* of salvation to all, or a vain attempt to "sell" Christ by begging sinners. The charisma and oratorical skill of the preacher are not the main thing in preaching, as so many seem to think today, but the fact that the preacher preaches nothing but Christ crucified as the power of God unto salvation. What one believes about the atonement, therefore, has a profound effect on the very nature and manner of gospel preaching.

2. Limited atonement and missions

The doctrine of limited atonement means that the calling of the church in missions is *not* to preach the gospel to every single soul now living but to preach it when and where God is pleased to send the gospel. It is a misunderstanding of this point that places a heavy burden of guilt on Christians today, for it is all but impossible, both in terms of cost and available manpower, to preach the gospel to every living human being. The church ought to feel guilty if Christ has died for every person and the church has not made that known to everyone living. Then there is no Christian living who ought not sell all his possessions and dedicate every moment of his life to try to accomplish this goal. If he does not, he is guilty of failing to let men know that Christ has died for them. Then, too, the church in the past has never realized her calling to preach the gospel to all the world, but has fallen far short of that most important calling of all: her great commission.

If, however, one believes in limited atonement, one can be sure that the cross is not for all. He will be satisfied to preach the gospel when and where God sends it. This is not to say that the church must not actively and aggressively do the work of missions, but only that she need not feel guilty when she is not able for legitimate reasons to bring the gospel to every single man, woman, and child. The church can rest content in the confidence that where God has His people, *He will* make it possible also for the church to preach the gospel, both by opening the door and by providing the necessary means.

3. Limited atonement and witnessing

Belief in limited atonement has an effect on the content of the believer's witness as well as the content of mission preaching. The doctrine of limited atonement means that neither the church in its mission preaching, nor the believer in his witnessing, may go to the lost and simply say to them, "Christ died for you!" To say that would in most cases be a lie, and the attempt to persuade the lost by telling them this would be little more than deception.

What the believer must do in his witnessing, and the church in her preaching, is to speak of Christ and the power of His work as well as the fact that He died for the sins of His people, calling the lost to repentance and faith in Christ and leaving the work of convincing and convicting sinners to the Holy Spirit.

4. Limited atonement and the assurance of salvation

It should be evident that our assurance of salvation depends on our knowing that the cross is salvation, full and free. If we should think that the cross was only a possibility of salvation, and that our benefiting from the cross was dependent on our accepting it, we would be bereft of all our comfort in Christ. Our comfort is the biblical truth that He is *all* our salvation and that *nothing* more is needed besides Him.

If we should think that God sincerely offered salvation to all men without exception, how would we ever know that we are *not* among those to whom salvation is sincerely offered by God but for whom God had not sent Christ? We must know that His blood is the only thing that stands between us and hell, for if that is not sufficient to save us, then what in all the world is?

5. Limited atonement and the glory of God

As far as glorifying and praising God in the church is concerned, limited atonement is also of the greatest possible value. Who can praise a God who sincerely offers salvation to all without even intending their salvation? Who could praise a

God who sent His Son into the world and subjected Him to the shame and reproach of the cross on the mere chance that some might be saved?

One thing is certain: however much some may quibble about these doctrines, God will not allow one drop of His Son's blood to be wasted or allow His costly death to be a failure. Nor will He allow His own wisdom to be impugned by the notion that He would go to such effort and pay such a price merely in the hope that some might be saved. He will not allow His power to be blasphemed as though He were not able to save all those whom He intended to save and for whom He sent His Son.

The sovereignty of God is really at stake here, and we ought to see that. God is not only sovereign in deciding from eternity who shall be saved, but He is the same sovereign God at the cross and in the preaching of the cross, for there, too, He decides who shall be saved and who shall profit from the blood of Jesus Christ His Son.

G. Relation to the other four points

The doctrine of limited atonement, as we have already to some extent seen, is inseparably related to the other four points of Calvinism. It is, therefore, really impossible to be a three- or four-point Calvinist and reject this doctrine while maintaining all or most of the others.

The connection between *unconditional* election and limited atonement is clear. Unconditional election explains what it is that limits the atonement, that is, the sovereign will and choice of God Himself. Universal atonement says that not God's will, but man's, limits the atonement and almost always, therefore, denies unconditional election, teaching instead a conditional election that God only *foresees* and then selects who will choose Christ and who will profit from Christ's death.

Election is in vain if salvation and the cross still depend on a man's freewill choice. Whether or not God chose anyone would make no difference. All would still hinge on man's decision to accept or reject Christ.

As far as total depravity is concerned, that doctrine is the reason why the atonement must be efficacious for all those whom God has given to Christ, for the doctrine of total depravity teaches us that man has of himself no power to accept Christ or to believe in the cross. If the power of the cross really depended on our acceptance of Christ, and if men are totally depraved, no one at all could possibly be saved by the cross.

Likewise, the doctrines of irresistible grace and perseverance follow from limited atonement. The doctrine of limited atonement means that Christ purchased everything by His death, including the grace that brings us to salvation and preserves us in salvation to the end. It also means that those for whom Christ died are saved and must be saved. It demands, therefore, a grace that is powerful and irresistible and that never fails.

CHAPTER V

Irresistible Grace

Does salvation depend on God's grace or on the sinner's free will? Can God's will to save man be frustrated? Can it happen that although God's grace has begun to work in a man, that grace is able to be resisted and lost? Does God merely *try* to save men, or does He *actually* save them?

These are vital questions! Their significance comes into no clearer focus than in a discussion of the truth of irresistible grace.

The doctrine of irresistible grace, or "efficacious grace" as it is sometimes referred to, is the fourth of the Five Points of Calvinism. It is represented by the *I* in the acronym *TULIP.* Irresistible grace stands opposed to the teaching that salvation depends on the final decision of man. According to Arminianism, God's grace can be frustrated by man. Calvinism teaches that God's grace irresistibly saves man.

By irresistible grace we mean that God's grace and salvation cannot be *effectively* resisted. When God determines to save a man, that man is saved! Neither that man himself nor the devil nor the wicked world are able to prevent his salvation. Nothing can stand in the way of God's saving purpose. Not only does God will to save him and work to save him, but He actually does save him, "For who hath resisted his will?" (Rom. 9:19).

Irresistible grace is an important issue. Let no church or individual Christian suppose otherwise. The importance of this issue is not merely that it concerns the question, "Can *grace* be resisted?" but ultimately the question, "Can *God* be resisted?" for the grace of salvation is *God's* grace. Can God, the sovereign God—the God about whom the Scriptures declare that "he doeth according to his will in the army of heaven . . . and none can stay his hand" (Dan. 4:35)—be frustrated in His will to save even one sinner? The issue concerns the very character and Being of God. The doctrine of irresistible grace confronts us with the most fundamental question with which a man can be faced: what do you believe about God?

Because the Reformed faith confesses the truth that God is a sovereign God, it also teaches the scriptural truth of His irresistible grace. This, surely, is rigorous logic, as any clear-thinking person can see. More importantly, this is the teaching of the Holy Scriptures. The purpose of this chapter will be to demonstrate the validity of this assertion.

A. The doctrine
1. Salvation due to the power of God's grace alone

If a sinner has been unconditionally elected to salvation in eternity by God the Father, in time he has been redeemed by the death of Jesus Christ. But this sinner must also be saved; that is, the benefits of Christ's death must be applied to him, and he must be made to possess the salvation that God has willed for him. He must be converted in heart and life from a dead, unbelieving, and disobedient sinner to a living, believing, and obedient child of God. The power of God that works this radical change in the sinner is *grace.*

Salvation is by grace, and by *grace* alone. In the history of the church this has proved to be the pivotal issue: *grace alone!* Always there have been those who, although they spoke of salvation by grace, also attributed salvation, at least to some extent, to the work and ability of man. Yes, salvation is due to the grace of God, they say (and still say!), but that grace of

God cooperates with the work and will of the sinner. Yes, the power of God accomplishes salvation, but the power of God depends on the willingness of the sinner. To sum up this view, salvation is due to the grace of God *and* something else, rather than to the grace of God *alone.*

The Scriptures teach quite definitely that salvation is by grace. In Ephesians 2:8 the apostle Paul teaches, "For by *grace* are ye saved through faith; and that not of yourselves: it is the gift of God." In Acts 20:24 the same apostle speaks of the gospel as "the gospel of the grace of God." Concerning himself, Paul says in 1 Corinthians 15:10, "By the grace of God I am what I am."

That we are saved by grace means that we are not saved by works. Salvation by grace alone means that our works do not at all contribute to our salvation. The fact that grace rules out works as the cause of salvation is plain from the Scriptures. We read in Romans 11:5, 6: "Even so then at this present time also there is a remnant according to the election of grace. And if by grace, then it is no more of works: otherwise grace is no more grace." Galatians 2:16 teaches the same truth: "Knowing that a man is not justified by the works of the law, but by the faith of Jesus Christ, even we have believed in Jesus Christ, that we might be justified by the faith of Christ, and not by the works of the law: for by the works of the law shall no flesh be justified." Paul declares in Titus 3:5, "Not by works of righteousness which we have done, but according to his mercy he saved us, by the washing of regeneration, and renewing of the Holy Ghost."

2. The *irresistible* grace of salvation

It is plain that the power of grace must be a great power. Man is the sinner; God must be the Savior. Man is incapable; God *must* be able. Man is powerless; God *must* be omnipotent. Man is weak; God *must* be sovereign.

We are like the man whom Jesus healed at the pool of Bethesda (John 5:1–9). Just as he was physically impotent, so are we spiritually impotent, absolutely unable to walk (spiritually) at all. And our condition is due to our sin, as was the case with the impotent man. "Afterward Jesus findeth him in the temple, and said unto him, Behold, thou art made whole: sin no more, lest a worse thing come unto thee" (John 5:14).

The saving of the sinner *demands* great power. The devil must be defeated; a rebel must be subdued; a heart of stone must be made a heart of flesh; a new creature must be brought forth; the dead must be raised. This work calls for great power, power that is beyond the power of a mere creature: miraculous power, supernatural power, divine power.

On the part of God, *great* power is required. Mere begging, pleading, or coaxing of men will not do. There must be the exercise of almighty power, such power as was exhibited in the creation of the world. Really every child of God is living evidence of the almighty power of God. On the part of anyone who has been the object of the saving grace of God, there can be no question of the sovereignty of God in salvation. Anyone who by God's grace knows himself, *knows* the sovereignty of God.

Granted that the power of grace is a great power, the question remains whether or not it is *irresistible* power. Granted that the sinner is dead, granted that God must work in salvation, granted that His work is powerful, could it not yet be that this work can be resisted and frustrated by the sinner? Could it not be that God works to give all men the ability to come to Christ *if* they choose to do so? Might not grace only *enable* men to come to Christ, always conditioned on their free will, so that man could very well choose *not* to come to Christ, and to *resist* His grace? The crucial question remains this: Is the grace of God *irresistible*?

The answer of the Scriptures and the Reformed faith is, Yes! Grace, if it is grace, must be irresistible grace. Because God is an irresistible, all powerful, totally sovereign God, His grace is irresistible, powerful, and sovereign. God and God's grace cannot effectively and ultimately be resisted by the most obstinate of sinners. When God's grace operates to save the sinner, that grace *will* triumph in the salvation of that sinner. He *will* be saved. God *will* have the victory. Not the power of the devil, not the power of the wicked world, not the power of the sinner himself, shall be able to prevent, overthrow, or frustrate the work of God's grace. The God of the Scriptures is the God of whom Isaiah says in Isaiah 46:10, 11, "I am God, and there is none like me, Declaring the end from the beginning, and from ancient times the things that are not yet done, saying, My counsel shall stand, and I will do all my pleasure." He is the God before whom Daniel says in Daniel 4:35, "All the inhabitants of the earth are reputed as nothing: and he doeth according to his will in the army of heaven, and among the inhabitants of the earth: and none can stay his hand, or say unto him, What doest thou?"

The god of resistible grace is not the God of the Scriptures. The former is a weak god, an ineffective god, a powerless god. In reality, he is no god at all, but an idol. This is the seriousness of the denial of God's irresistible grace!

B. Scripture proofs

What Bible passages prove this teaching of irresistible grace? Do the Scriptures support this teaching? Without doubt, they do.

1. Salvation by grace alone
   a. Romans 3:24: "Being justified freely by his grace through the redemption that is in Christ Jesus."

b. Romans 4:16: "Therefore it [salvation] is of faith, that it might be by grace; to the end the promise might be sure to all the seed."

c. Romans 9:16: "So then it [salvation] is not of him that willeth ["free" will], nor of him that runneth ["good" works], but of *God* that sheweth mercy."

d. 1 Corinthians 15:10: "By the grace of God I am what I am: and his grace which was bestowed upon me was not in vain; but I laboured more abundantly than they all: yet not I, but the grace of God which was with me."

e. Ephesians 2:8: "For by grace are ye saved through faith; and that not of yourselves: it is the gift of God."

2. Salvation *not* by man's works

a. Romans 3:28: "Therefore we conclude that a man is justified by faith without the deeds of the law."

b. Romans 11:6: "And if by grace, then it is no more of works: otherwise grace is no more grace. But if it be of works, then is it no more grace: otherwise work is no more work."

c. Galatians 5:4: "Christ is become of no effect unto you, whosoever of you are justified by the law; ye are fallen from grace."

d. Ephesians 2:8, 9: "For by grace are ye saved through faith; and that not of yourselves: it is the gift of God: *Not of works, lest any man should boast.*"

e. 2 Timothy 1:9: "Who hath saved us, and called us with an holy calling, not according to our works, but according to His own purpose and grace, which was given us in Christ Jesus before the world began."

f. Titus 3:5: "Not by works of righteousness which we have done, but according to his mercy he saved us, by the washing of regeneration, and renewing of the Holy Ghost."

3. Repenting and believing by the grace of God
   a. John 3:27: "John [the Baptist] answered and said, A man can receive nothing, except it be given him from heaven."
   b. John 6:65: "And he said, Therefore said I unto you, that no man can come unto me, except it were given unto him of my Father."
   c. Acts 5:31: "Him hath God exalted with his right hand to be a Prince and a Saviour, for to *give* repentance to Israel, and forgiveness of sins."
   d. Acts 11:18: "When they heard these things, they held their peace, and glorified God, saying, Then hath God also to the Gentiles *granted* repentance unto life."
   e. Acts 16:14: "And a certain woman named Lydia, a seller of purple, of the city of Thyatira, which worshipped God, heard us: whose heart *the Lord* opened, that she attended unto the things which were spoken of Paul."
   f. Acts 18:27: "And when he [Apollos] was disposed to pass into Achaia, the brethren wrote, exhorting the disciples to receive him: who, when he was come, helped them much which had believed *through grace*."
   g. 1 Corinthians 4:7: "For who maketh thee to differ from another? and what hast thou that thou didst not receive? now if thou didst receive it, why dost thou glory, as if thou hadst not received it?"
   h. Philippians 1:29: "For unto you it is *given* in the behalf of Christ, not only to believe on him, but also to suffer for his sake."

i. Philippians 2:13: "For *it is God which worketh in you* both *to will* and *to do* of his good pleasure."

j. 2 Timothy 2:25: "In meekness instructing those that oppose themselves; if God peradventure will *give* them repentance to the acknowledging of the truth."

4. *Irresistible* grace

That the grace of salvation is irresistible is the clear teaching of the multitude of Scripture passages that speak of God efficaciously saving sinners. God does not try to save sinners, depending on their cooperation. He does not attempt to save sinners but stand helplessly by unless they at least exercise their free will. He does not do His best to save sinners, always facing the real possibility that His best is not good enough and that the sinner may effectively resist His efforts to save him. No, God *saves* sinners sovereignly, efficaciously, irresistibly. *This* is the language of the Scriptures from beginning to end.

a. Deuteronomy 30:6: "And the LORD thy God *will circumcise* thine heart, and the heart of thy seed, to love the LORD thy God with all thine heart, and with all thy soul, that thou mayest live."

b. Isaiah 55:11: "So shall my word be that goeth forth out of my mouth: it shall not return unto me void, but it shall accomplish that which I please, and it shall prosper in the thing whereunto I sent it."

c. Ezekiel 36:26, 27: "A new heart also *will I give* you, and a new spirit *will I put* within you: and *I will take away* the stony heart out of your flesh, and *I will give* you an heart of flesh. And *I will put* my spirit within you, and *cause you to walk* in my statutes, and ye *shall keep* my judgments, and *do* them."

d. John 6:37: "All that the Father giveth me [Jesus] shall come to me; and him that cometh to me I will in no wise cast out."

e. John 6:39: "And this is the Father's will which hath sent me, that of all which he hath given me I should lose nothing, but should raise it up again at the last day."

f. John 6:44, 45: "No man can come to me, except the Father which hath sent me draw him: and I will raise him up at the last day. It is written in the prophets, And they shall be all taught of God. Every man therefore that hath heard, and hath learned of the Father, cometh unto me."

g. Romans 8:29, 30: "For whom he did foreknow [loved before time began], he also did predestinate to be conformed to the image of his Son, that he might be the firstborn among many brethren. Moreover whom he did predestinate, them he also called: and whom he called, them he also justified: and whom he justified, them he also glorified."

All who are predestinated (the elect) and called by God are infallibly brought to salvation. The result of their being predestinated and called is that they *are justified* and *glorified*. *Nothing* can prevent the final glorification of any who are predestinated and called.

5. Salvation as rebirth, re-creation, resurrection

The Scriptures' description of salvation as rebirth, re-creation, and resurrection from the dead, leaves beyond question the truth of irresistible grace.

a. Rebirth

Over and over again the Bible speaks of salvation as a rebirth. This is Jesus' description of salvation in His well-known discourse with Nicodemus in John 3. In the third verse Jesus says, "Verily, verily, I say unto thee, Except a man be born again, he cannot see the kingdom of God." Other Scriptures that refer to salvation as a rebirth include John 1:13; John 5:21, 24; Ephesians 1:19, 20; Ephesians 2:1, 5; Colossians 2:13; Titus 3:5; 1 Peter 1:3; 1 John 2:29; 1 John 3:9; 1 John 4:7; 1 John 5:1, 4, 18.

The fact that salvation is a rebirth implies that the grace of salvation is irresistible. As far as physical birth is concerned, the child who is born has no say in the matter of whether or not he will be born. He does not cooperate in being born, does not even will to be conceived and brought forth. Neither is he able effectively to resist conception and birth. What is true of physical birth is also true of spiritual rebirth. It is not due to us; we do not cooperate in it, nor are we able effectively to resist it.

b. Re-creation

Often the Scriptures describe our salvation in terms of re-creation. Paul writes, for example, in 2 Corinthians 5:17, "Therefore if any man be in Christ, he is a new creature: old things are passed away; behold, all things are become new." Other places in the Scriptures where this figure is employed include Galatians 6:15; Ephesians 2:10; Ephesians 4:24; Colossians 3:10.

That salvation is a re-creation also implies that the grace of salvation is irresistible. Just ask yourself: "When God created all things in the beginning, how did He create them? Did He create them in such a way that when He spoke the creative word calling each creature into being, it still remained a question whether or not that creature would actually come into being? Did the creature cooperate with God in its creation? Was there a single creature able to resist God's creative word? To ask these questions is to answer them. What was true of God's original creation of all things in the beginning is also true of His still greater work of re-creation.

c.   Resurrection

Still another common figure used in the Scriptures to describe God's work of saving lost sinners is resurrection from the dead. Recall the well-known prophecy of the dry bones in Ezekiel 37. In Ephesians 2:1 Paul writes, "And you hath he quickened [made alive again], who were dead in trespasses and sins." Other Scripture passages where this same figure occurs include John 5:28, 29; Romans 6:13; Romans 8:10; Romans 11:15; Ephesians 2:5; Colossians 2:13; Colossians 3:1.

The saving of the sinner is a resurrection of the sinner, a resurrecting of him from spiritual death, a raising of him from his being dead in trespasses and sins. By describing salvation as a resurrection from death, the Bible emphasizes that the power that saves the sinner is an irresistible power. It is folly to teach that the work of salvation is due to the cooperation of the sinner. It is folly to teach that in the work of salvation the sinner is able to frustrate and resist God's intentions and work of saving him. Can a dead man cooperate in his being made alive? Could Lazarus have frustrated Christ's intentions of raising him from the dead? In the last day, when Christ comes again and raises the dead, will those dead bodies be in a position to cooperate in being raised or to refuse to be raised, resisting the power of the resurrection and preventing the will of the exalted Christ that they be raised? Of course not. Neither is the sinner able to cooperate in or resist God's salvation of him.

6. The sovereignty of God's will

Those texts of the Scriptures that teach the sovereignty of God's will also imply the truth of irresistible grace. If that which God wills always comes to pass, then God's purpose to save a sinner is a purpose that must be realized.

a. Psalm 115:3: "But our God is in the heavens: he hath done whatsoever he hath pleased."

b. Isaiah 46:9, 10: "Remember the former things of old: for I am God, and there is none else; I am God, and there is none like me, Declaring the end from the beginning, and from ancient times the things that are not yet done, saying, My counsel shall stand, and I will do all my pleasure."

c. Daniel 4:35: "And all the inhabitants of the earth are reputed as nothing: and he doeth according to his will in the army of heaven, and among the inhabitants of the earth: and none can stay his hand, or say unto him, What doest thou?"

C. Difficult passages

Against the doctrine of irresistible grace, appeal is often made to certain passages of Scripture that seem to teach it is indeed possible for the sinner to resist and thus frustrate the grace of God.

In explanation of these passages let it be understood that the doctrine of irresistible grace does not mean that the natural man does not stand opposed to God, God's Christ, God's Spirit, and God's Word. He certainly does. He is a rebel against God and a hater of God. There is no love of God in him nor desire to please God. This is simply what it means that the sinner is totally depraved. In this sense it certainly is true that the sinner resists God and salvation.

But the question is, Can the sinner *effectively* resist God's grace? Can he maintain his resistance against God even when God has determined to save and has begun to save him? Can he frustrate the Holy Spirit when once the Spirit has begun to work in his heart and life? The answer to all these questions is, No! In this sense, God cannot be resisted. His grace is an irresistible grace.

1. Matthew 23:37: Jesus laments, "O Jerusalem, Jerusalem, thou that killest the prophets, and stonest them which are sent unto thee, how often would I have gathered thy children together, even as a hen gathereth her chickens under her wings, and ye would not!"

In the verse above, we read the lament of Jesus over Jerusalem. Yes, the wicked leaders of the Jews did everything they could to prevent Jesus' gathering of Jerusalem's children. They stoned the prophets and opposed Jesus' preaching and teaching. They discredited Jesus before the people and threatened reprisal against any who openly confessed Him. In no way does this imply, however, that these wicked leaders succeeded in preventing Jesus from gathering Jerusalem's children. The elect of Jerusalem's children were gathered and saved, not withstanding the resistance of the wicked rulers.

2. Acts 7:51: "Ye do always resist the Holy Ghost: as your fathers did, so do ye."

Stephen's accusation against the unbelieving Jews was that their fathers had always resisted the Holy Ghost, and so did they. This does not imply that grace is resistible. Stephen is not talking about these wicked Jews effectively resisting the grace of the Holy Spirit working within them to save them. Not at all! He is rather talking about their opposition to the Holy Spirit in the sense that they constantly opposed the Word of the Holy Spirit in the Scriptures and the prophets who were the instruments of the Holy Spirit to bring that Word. As their fathers resisted Moses and Aaron, so did the Jews of Stephen's day resist Jesus and His apostles. They did not resist the Holy Spirit within them, for they were devoid of the Holy Spirit. The proof of that is their rejection and stoning of Stephen. But their resistance was to the external call, commands, reproofs, and teaching of the servants of God sent by the Spirit.

D. Objections
1. "Irresistible grace means that man is saved against his will."

Against the Scripture's teaching of irresistible grace, the enemies of this truth raise several objections. One of their objections is that if God's grace is irresistible, then man is actually saved contrary to his will. Caricaturing Calvinism, they say it teaches that Christ draws sinners kicking and screaming into heaven, that God forces men against their wills to be saved. Those who hold to irresistible grace are charged with teaching that God deals with men as senseless stocks, blocks, or puppets.

We reject this charge! This is not the teaching of the Bible but a gross misrepresentation.

Neither is it the case that one defends the truth of sovereign grace by denying or downplaying the activity of faith. One does not show himself to be a staunch advocate of irresistible grace by getting nervous whenever someone speaks of *our* repenting, *our* believing, or *our* coming to Christ, as if this puts the emphasis on man, man's work, and man's ability, and jeopardizes the truth of sovereign grace.

The reality is that the fruit, the infallible effect of God's grace in the sinner, is that although he once did not believe in Jesus Christ, now he believes in the true Jesus Christ. Although before he did not repent of his sins, now he truly repents of his sins. Although before he would not come to the true Christ, now he wills and actually does come to Christ. Irresistible grace does not rule out repentance and faith but rather guarantees that the sinner will repent and will believe in Jesus Christ.

We have an illustration of this truth in Jesus' miraculous healing of the lame man at the pool of Bethesda in John 5. That impotent man had absolutely no ability in himself to walk, nor was he in any position to cooperate with Jesus in the miracle of his healing. But when Jesus spoke the word that healed him, that impotent man was healed, and the effect of his being healed was that he did what he could not do before: he took up his bed and walked.

That our willing and doing are the effect of God's grace at work in our lives is plainly taught in Scripture. David declares in Psalm 110:3, "Thy people shall be willing in the day of thy power." Paul writes, "For it is God which worketh in you both to will and to do of his good pleasure" (Phil. 2:13).

2. "Irresistible grace makes preaching and the other means of grace unnecessary."

Another objection against the truth of irresistible grace is that it effectively rules out the use of means, particularly the means of the preaching of the gospel. If man does not have the ability in himself to believe, to accept Jesus Christ and salvation, why call men to faith in Jesus Christ? If it does not lie in the ability of every man to cooperate in salvation, why preach the gospel to all men? If God's grace is irresistible and if the will of God to save certain men will certainly come to pass, why should the church be concerned to preach the gospel at home or on the mission field? Will not God save his people regardless?

This objection does violence to the truth that although God's grace is irresistible, that irresistible grace of God is worked in men *through definite means,* chief of which is the preaching of the gospel. The divine rule in this matter is that God works and maintains His grace in the hearts of His elect people by the means of gospel preaching.

The warning of the Canons of Dordt, III/IV, Article 17, is in order here: "As the almighty operation of God, whereby he prolongs and supports this our natural life, does not exclude, but requires the use of means, by which God of his infinite mercy and goodness hath chosen to exert his influence, so also the beforementioned supernatural operation of God, by which we are regenerated, in no wise excludes, or subverts the use of the gospel, which the most wise God has ordained to be the seed of regeneration, and food of the soul. Wherefore, as the apostles, and teachers who succeeded them, piously instructed the people concerning this grace of God, to his glory, and the abasement of all pride, and in the meantime, however, neglected not to keep them by the sacred precepts of the gospel in the exercise of the Word, sacraments and discipline; so, even to this day, be it far from either instructors or instructed to presume to tempt God in the church by separating what he of his good pleasure hath most intimately joined together."

E. Denials of irresistible grace
1. Free will

The outstanding denial of irresistible grace is the popular teaching concerning the "free will" of the sinner. Those who hold to free will not only teach that man has the ability within himself to accept Jesus Christ, but they also teach that it is in the power of every man to reject Jesus Christ, that is, to resist and frustrate the operations of God's grace and to prevent Christ's efforts to save him. What blasphemy!

This was the teaching by Erasmus at the time of the Reformation concerning the power of free will. In his book *On the Freedom of the Will,* Erasmus states, "By free choice in this place we mean a power of the human will by which a man can apply himself to the things which lead to eternal salvation, or turn away from them."[1]

The Arminians at the Synod of Dordt ascribed the same power to free will. To the Synod they stated their position as follows: "Nevertheless we do not believe that all zeal, care, and diligence exerted to obtain salvation before faith itself and the Spirit of regeneration, are idle and in vain, yea, even much rather harmful to man, but useful and profitable; on the contrary, we hold that to hear God's Word, to be sorry for sins committed, to desire the saving grace of God and the Spirit of regeneration (with which things nevertheless man is able to do nothing without grace) not only are not harmful and unprofitable, but much rather altogether useful and highly necessary in order to obtain faith and the Spirit of renewal."[2]

Although the statements of Erasmus and of the Arminians were somewhat guarded, the greatest claims for free will are made today. Almost unlimited power is ascribed to the will of the sinner. Free will is able to accept Jesus Christ offered in the gospel, is mighty to open up the heart to a pleading Savior, is capable of making a decision for God. Indeed, free will is more powerful than God Himself, for it can resist God and prevent the operations of God's saving grace.

It ought to be clear that to teach free will is to deny irresistible grace. If the power of free will is not only that it can accept Jesus Christ and salvation but also reject the same, man is able effectively to resist God' grace. If God desires the salvation of all men, but salvation depends on the exercise of his free will, it is necessarily implied that although God desires the salvation of a certain man, that man may be able to frustrate God's desire to save him.

In fact, not only is the teaching of free will a denial of the irresistible character of God's grace, it is really a denial of grace altogether. If salvation depends on a power in man, a power that is able either to accept or to reject salvation, salvation becomes a work of man. And if salvation is due to a work of man, however small that work may be, it is not any longer due to the grace of God.

If man through his so-called free will is able to defeat God's will in salvation, then man becomes a god—falling prey to Satan's lie: "Ye shall be as gods" (Gen. 3:5). And if we are gods, then God is not God alone. Free will is deadly serious!

2. Synergism

Synergism is a word derived from the combination of two Greek words that literally mean *working together.* In theology, synergism refers to the view that man and God cooperate in salvation. Specifically, it teaches that the will of man cooperates with the Spirit of God in the work of regeneration.

Synergism is basically the same as the teaching of free willl, with the one refinement that salvation is not due *exclusively* to the exercise of man's free will, but to the cooperation of man's will *and* God's will. The initial work of salvation is accomplished jointly by God and man.

The teaching of synergism is also a denial of irresistible grace. It is a denial of the sinfulness and spiritual deadness of man, who is the object of God's grace. It is a denial also of the sovereign and irresisble character of God's grace, making the effectiveness of the grace of God dependent on the cooperation of sinful man.

3. Common grace

The teaching of common grace leads to a denial of irresistible grace. That is not hard to demonstrate. Common grace is a grace of God that is shown to all men but does not save them. To teach a non-saving grace of God, to teach a grace of God of which all men are the objects, is the first step towards outright denial of irresistible grace. In fact, in those churches in which common grace has become accepted dogma, there has been a weakening and even on occasion open renunciation of the doctrine of irresistible grace.

4. The free offer of the gospel

The teaching of the free offer of the gospel, inasmuch as it presupposes the free will of the sinner, is also an implicit denial of the irresistibility of grace. If the gospel is not any longer the power of God unto salvation, as Paul says that it is in Romans 1:16, and if it is not the means by which God works grace in the hearts of the elect, but only an *offer* of salvation dependent on the sinner's acceptance of that offer, then it is surely implied that the sinner may very well choose to reject the gospel and the offer of grace and salvation in that gospel. Then, although God wants to save him, although God expresses His love for him in the gospel, the sinner is able to frustrate that desire and love of God. The doctrine of irresistible grace is thereby negated.

F. Practical importance

The importance of the doctrine of irresistible grace is great. It belongs to the message of the gospel. From various points of view, it is important for the church and for every Christian personally to hold to this truth.

1. Irresistible grace and salvation by grace

The maintaining of irresistible grace is important for our confession of the truth that salvation is of grace. To deny irresistible grace, to teach free will, is to teach that salvation depends upon the will and work of man. It is to teach grace *plus* works rather than grace alone. That is not *the* gospel, but another gospel, a false gospel, a gospel that is no gospel at all.

2. Irresistible grace and assurance of salvation

The believer's assurance depends on the truth of irresistible grace. If it is possible that God's grace can be resisted, that after God has begun his saving work in me, it is still possible that I can resist it and lose it, how can I ever be sure of my salvation? I cannot be. The doctrine of free will and the teaching of resistible grace are cruel doctrines. They strip the child of God of the assurance of salvation. Then he must live in constant doubt and fear whether he will ever be saved. That is frightening! That is paralyzing! That is depressing!

3. Irresistible grace and intercessory prayer

If God's grace were not irresistible, it would be foolish to pray for the conversion or repentance of anyone. If God stands by powerlessly before the dread majesty of man's free will, what sense would there be to pray for Him to convert anyone. What despair for the Christian married to an unbelieving mate! What despair for those believing parents who have a wayward child! What despair for that church that has straying members! On the other hand, what hope we may have when we understand that the grace of God is sovereign and irresistible! Each of God's people know this by experience.

G. Relation to the other four points

Certainly the truth of irresistible grace establishes the truth of the sovereignty of God. If God is sovereign, and He is, the grace of God must be an irresistible grace. To deny irresistible grace is really to deny the sovereignty of God. Then God and God's will are dependent on man and man's will. Then Christ is reduced to a beggar. The Holy Spirit is a weakling. God is put in the position of Darius who earnestly desired to save Daniel from the lion's den, but could not (Dan. 6). Because God is God, the almighty God, His grace is irresistible grace.

Irresistible grace is necessitated by man's total depravity. Exactly because man is a sinner, unworthy of salvation, his salvation must be by grace. And since man is such a sinner that there is no good in him, no ability for good, no desire even for good, the grace of salvation must be an irresistible grace.

Unconditional election establishes the basis for irresistible grace. As God's salvation of men eternally did not rest on any worth or works in those men, and was completely unconditional, so His salvation of them in time does not rest on any of their worth or works. And that is exactly the teaching of irresistible grace.

Irresistible grace preserves the truth of limited atonement. If free will and resistible grace are true, it would be possible that Christ died in vain. Then, although Christ died for a man and wants to save that man, He would be frustrated because of the unwillingness of the sinner to be saved.

Irresistible grace also guarantees the preservation of the saints. Since the grace of God that brings salvation to a man is a sovereign, almighty grace, the grace of God that continues to abide in a man is a sovereign, almighty grace also. Just as it cannot be frustrated in its initial operations, neither can it be frustrated ultimately. Those who are brought to salvation by the irresistible grace of God are, by the power of that same grace, preserved in salvation unto the end.

CHAPTER VI

The Perseverance of the Saints

The last of the Five Points of Calvinism is represented by
the letter *P* in the word *TULIP* and is the doctrine of the
perseverance of the saints. This doctrine deals with the question whether those who are once brought to faith and salvation will continue in faith and in that salvation to the very end,
in other words, whether those who once believe will finally
and surely go to heaven.

Some who call themselves Calvinists have reservations
about this doctrine, and some reject it altogether, though they
may accept the rest of the Five Points. At times this is due to
a misunderstanding of the doctrine, and it is our hope and
prayer that our presentation of it will not contribute to those
misunderstandings but make as clear as possible what the
Bible teaches.

A. The name

There are three different names used for this doctrine.

1. The perseverance of saints

The name used in the Canons of Dordt, the original Five
Points of Calvinism, is "the perseverance of the saints." This

name, as we shall see, emphasizes the *responsibility* of every believer to continue or "persevere" in faith and holiness.

2. The preservation of saints

Many Calvinists prefer to speak of "the preservation of the saints" because this name emphasizes the same thing that the other points emphasize, that is, the sovereignty of God in salvation and the truth that salvation is *all* of grace from beginning to end. This name, then, teaches the truth that God "preserves" all those whom He has chosen and redeemed and in whose hearts He has worked by the power of His irresistible grace.

3. Eternal security

The third name that is used for this doctrine is "eternal security." This emphasizes the comfort that believers receive from the doctrine: that they are secure in their salvation, not only through this life but into eternity.

This name, while not in itself objectionable, is often used by those who believe "once saved, always saved," no matter how a person lives or what he does. That teaching, as we hope to show, is not biblical, and if we use the name "eternal security," we must be sure to contradict that teaching. We may not believe that the assurance of final salvation allows anyone to live carelessly and wickedly.

B. The doctrine

Whatever name is used for this doctrine, it teaches that all those who receive salvation can never again lose it or fall away from it. They are "once saved, always saved." The words "perseverance," "preservation," and "eternal security" all emphasize this.

1. Saints

When we speak of the perseverance or preservation of *saints,* we are teaching the truth that those who are saved persevere to the end as a result of the grace of God, not as a result of their own strength or works, but always in the way of real, personal holiness.

The name "saints," when it is applied to believers (as it is in almost all of the epistles of Paul, such as Romans 1:7, 1 Corinthians 1:2, 2 Corinthians 1:1, Ephesians 1:1, and Philippians 1:1) is a name that refers to their holiness. The name means *holy ones.* It is very important for our study that this word is included. We do not believe just in perseverance or preservation, but in the perseverance of *saints.* It is important, first of all, because it reminds us of the real issue. The question raised by this doctrine is not simply whether or not the Bible teaches that a person once saved is always saved, but also what the Bible teaches about saints. Our definition of a saint will probably determine whether or not we believe in this doctrine and how we interpret the teaching of the Scriptures. If a saint is a self-made person, that is, one who has made himself holy or who is able to be holy by his own strength, then, obviously, whether or not he will always be holy also depends on him, whether or not he will continue to keep himself holy.

The Bible, however, shows that saints are holy *only* by the grace of God, that of themselves they are sinners and have no natural holiness or power to be holy. It is God who makes saints. So, too, if saints are made by God, their continuing in holiness also depends on Him and on His grace, and not on themselves.

If you define a saint, therefore, as one who is chosen unconditionally from eternity, whose sins are fully paid for by the blood of the atonement, and who is inwardly regenerated and renewed by the irresistible power of the Holy Spirit, then it is impossible to believe in anything else but the preservation and perseverance of that same saint.

2. Preservation

The name "preservation of the saints" emphasizes that God by His grace and in His goodness sovereignly and eternally preserves those in whose hearts He has begun to work and finally brings them to glory in Christ. Thus, the doctrine is only an extension of the doctrine of irresistible grace, for it is that same irresistible grace that preserves and keeps safe God's saints and brings them to glory. To deny perseverance is to teach that God's work can come to nothing and His power be thwarted—that His grace is not, after all, irresistible.

3. Perseverance

However, that God sovereignly preserves His chosen and redeemed saints does not take away their responsibility to live holy and thankful lives. True Calvinism has never taught this. God does preserve His people in salvation, but always in such a way that they also persevere in holiness. The Canons of Dordt use the name "perseverance of the saints" to make it as clear as possible that this doctrine does not give His saints the excuse to be anything but saints in their conduct. It is emphatically *saints* who are preserved by the grace of God. Those who are unholy, wicked, and profane do not, and cannot, have the hope of being preserved.

4. Falling, but not falling away

On the other hand, this doctrine does not mean that God's saints never fall into sin or temptation. The very names that are used, "preservation" and "perseverance," imply that God's people are surrounded by spiritual dangers and enemies and that they themselves are always liable to fall into temptation and to be overcome by their enemies, the devil, the wicked world, and their own sinfulness. The doctrine means that as far as God is concerned, He never allows them to fall away completely or to lose their salvation but always brings them back. As far as they are concerned, it means that they, by the grace of God, always come again to repentance and begin anew the struggle to be holy. The parables of the lost sheep and of the prodigal son are illustrations of what this doctrine teaches, the former parable teaching especially the preserving power of God in and through Jesus Christ our Shepherd, and the latter parable demonstrating our perseverance in the way of repentance and spiritual renewal.

In summary, then, this doctrine teaches the following:

    a. Saints are such by election, atonement, and sovereign grace.
    b. They cannot, therefore, be lost.
    c. This assurance of eternal salvation does not remove the obligation they have to live as saints in the world, holy and obedient.
    d. They must be preserved and must persevere exactly because of their own weakness and sinfulness and because of their spiritual enemies, the devil and the wicked world.

C. Scripture proofs

As always, it is necessary to show that this doctrine is biblical, as indeed it is, being taught both in the Old and the New Testaments.

1. Passages that speak of preservation
   a. Psalm 37:23, 24: "The steps of a good man are ordered by the LORD: and he delighteth in his way. Though he fall, he shall not be utterly cast down: for the LORD upholdeth him with his hand."

This passage reminds us that it is possible for God's people to fall into sin and temptation, but in contrast also speaks of the impossibility of their falling away completely and ascribes this not only to the power of God, but also to His eternal decree ("The steps of a good man are *ordered* by the Lord").

   b. Psalm 37:28: "For the LORD loveth judgment, and forsaketh not his saints; they are preserved forever: but the seed of the wicked shall be cut off."

The Psalm again speaks both of preservation and of the fact that it is the saints who are preserved. It also teaches that this depends on God. The saints are "his," and they are preserved because God in His faithfulness does not forsake them. He does not forsake them, because *He* is righteous—not because *they* are. Their preservation does not depend on themselves.

   c. Isaiah 45:17: "But Israel shall be saved in the LORD with an everlasting salvation: ye shall not be ashamed nor confounded world without end."

Perhaps even more important than this passage itself is the context, which grounds the assurance of salvation in the power of God and insists (v. 19) that to say otherwise would make God's call powerless and Himself unrighteous and a liar, for He would then be promising what He Himself is unable to give.

   d. Isaiah 49:16: "Behold, I have graven thee upon the palms of my hands; thy walls are continually before me."

Not only does this verse connect election and preservation in a most beautiful way, speaking as though the names of God's people are actually engraved eternally in the palms of His hands, but it also assures God's people of this in answer to their fears. The verse is an answer to Zion's complaint: "The LORD hath forsaken me, and my Lord hath forgotten me" (v. 14), a complaint often heard in times of trouble.

   e. Jeremiah 32:40: "And I will make an everlasting covenant with them, that I will not turn away from them, to do them good; but I will put my fear in their hearts, that they shall not depart from me."

Jeremiah's message is particularly important because it makes Israel's restoration after the captivity a figure and type of the preservation of the church in every age, assuring the people of God that the fruit of grace will be that they will not turn away from Him. Jeremiah shows, therefore, the connection between the grace of God that preserves and the resultant perseverance of the saints.

   f. Luke 22:31, 32: "And the Lord said, Simon, Simon, behold, Satan hath desired to have you, that he may sift you as wheat: But I have prayed for thee, that thy faith fail not: and when thou art converted, strengthen thy brethren."

Christ not only assures Peter, and with him every one of us, that He will pray for Peter in time of temptation, knowing already what will happen, but He also tells Peter, even before he falls, that he will be converted again in answer to His prayer.

> g. John 3:16: "For God so loved the world, that he gave his only begotten Son, that whosoever believeth in him should not perish, but have everlasting life."

Strangely enough, this verse, which is so often quoted by those who believe that salvation and eternal life depend on the choice of man's own will, actually teaches the very opposite, namely, that those who believe *shall not perish,* but through faith *have* everlasting life. That could not be true unless faith, like eternal life, was God's unchangeable gift and not man's changeable choice. Similar passages are John 3:36 and John 5:24.

> h. John 6:39: "And this is the Father's will which hath sent me, that of all which he hath given me I should lose nothing, but should raise it up again at the last day."

Jesus shows the connection between election and the atonement. He actually saves (does not lose) those whom the Father gave Him, and He does that according to the Father's own will. He also shows the connection between both of those doctrines and preservation. Those whom the Father gave Him and whom He does not lose shall be raised up again on the last day. We have, then, from Jesus Himself, a very beautiful and powerful reminder that the guarantee of perseverance and eternal security is not our faithfulness, but God's grace in election and in the cross.

> i. John 10:27–29: "My sheep hear my voice, and I know them, and they follow me: And I give unto

them eternal life; and they shall never perish, neither shall any man pluck them out of my hand. My Father, which gave them me, is greater than all; and no man is able to pluck them out of my Father's hand."

This passage grounds the preservation of saints in election ("I know them") and in the almighty power of God that cannot be thwarted ("My Father . . . is greater than all"). In the context, which speaks of Jesus as the shepherd of the sheep, it also shows that these sheep are preserved and must be preserved, because the blood of the good shepherd was shed for them. Nor may we overlook the fact that through all this, the sheep follow Jesus. They are not preserved to walk in their own way, but in holiness of life and obedience to Jesus.

> j. John 17:11: "And now I am no more in the world, but these are in the world, and I come to thee. Holy Father, keep through thine own name those whom thou hast given me, that they may be one, as we are."
>
> k. John 17:24: "Father, I will that they also, whom thou hast given me, be with me where I am; that they may behold my glory, which thou hast given me: for thou lovedst me before the foundation of the world."

In light of Luke 22:32, which shows that Jesus' prayers on behalf of His people are surely answered, the verses above are most significant. Jesus is not only praying that His people may be preserved in the world (v. 11), but also to final heavenly glory. So we see that the preservation of the saints is the result also of the perfect intercession of Christ, which would be revealed as powerless and ineffectual if they were lost.

l. Romans 8:35–39: "Who shall separate us from the love of Christ? shall tribulation, or distress, or persecution, or famine, or nakedness, or peril, or sword? As it is written, For thy sake we are killed all the day long; we are accounted as sheep for the slaughter. Nay, in all these things we are more than conquerors through him that loved us. For I am persuaded, that neither death, nor life, nor angels, nor principalities, nor powers, nor things present, nor things to come, Nor height, nor depth, nor any other creature, shall be able to separate us from the love of God, which is in Christ Jesus our Lord."

Paul assures believers of three things: first, that persecution and other such trials will not cause them to be separated from Christ; second, that neither will spiritual powers, including the devil himself, be able to do that; and third, that this is true because of the love of God in Christ, which is revealed in the death of Christ, in His resurrection and intercession, and in our justification before God (vv. 29–34). Once again we are taught that for saints to fall away, the cross and intercession of Christ would have to be made of none effect and the love and grace of God become powerless.

m. 1 Corinthians 1:7–9: "So that ye come behind in no gift; waiting for the coming of our Lord Jesus Christ: Who shall confirm you unto the end, that ye may be blameless in the day of our Lord Jesus Christ. God is faithful, by whom ye were called in the fellowship of his Son Jesus Christ our Lord."

That we are confirmed unto the end is simply an evidence of the faithfulness of God who called us. Not to be confirmed unto the end and unto blamelessness would be unfaithfulness on God's part, not just to us, but to Himself and His own work, for He called us. We, of course, are always unfaithful and fail, but God's faithfulness never fails.

> n. 2 Corinthians 4:8–10: "We are troubled on every side, yet not distressed; we are perplexed, but not in despair; Persecuted, but not forsaken; cast down, but not destroyed; Always bearing about in the body the dying of the Lord Jesus, that the life also of Jesus might be made manifest in our body."

Here we learn that the perseverance of the saints does not mean that God's people are preserved from all troubles, trials, and temptations, but that God protects them in their tribulations and brings them safely through. We persevere through many dangers.

> o. Philippians 1:6: "Being confident of this very thing, that he which hath begun a good work in you will perform it until the day of Jesus Christ."

Again, the perseverance of saints is ascribed to the faithfulness of God and the work of God. The fact that salvation is of grace at the beginning means that it is all of grace and shall certainly be finished in all those in whom it is begun.

> p. 2 Timothy 2:19: "Nevertheless the foundation of God standeth sure, having this seal, The Lord knoweth them that are his. And, Let every one that nameth the name of Christ depart from iniquity."

This assured statement is made in the face of the evil work of those who had been troubling the church and had even "overthrown the faith of some" (v. 18). "Nevertheless," that is, even though it might have appeared that some had lost faith and salvation, the foundation of God stands sure. What God has worked cannot be defeated or destroyed.

In spite of the strong language used to describe the defection of some, the verse leads to two conclusions: that those whose "faith" was overthrown did not have true faith, the faith God gives; and that those who had true faith could not, and would not, lose it.

We are reminded, however, that the seal that guarantees that God's foundation and work cannot perish is election ("the Lord knoweth them that are his"). The other side of that seal, however, says, "Let every one that nameth the name of the LORD depart from iniquity." Sanctification of heart and life is part of preservation. Indeed, it is the guarantee *in our own lives,* the subjective and temporal guarantee that God has begun His work and will not forsake it, just as election is the objective and eternal guarantee.

> q. 2 Timothy 4:18: "And the Lord shall deliver me from every evil work, and will preserve me unto his heavenly kingdom: to whom be glory for ever and ever. Amen."

No one would dare to say this if his future glory depended in any way on himself, and no one would be able to say it if he did not know that God in His faithfulness does preserve His people.

> r. Hebrews 7:25: "Wherefore he is able also to save them to the uttermost that come unto God by him, seeing he ever liveth to make intercession for them."

This Word of God connects our preservation and Christ's intercession. Remember, though, that it is not only Christ's prayers that fail if any of those who are saved fall away, but also His blood that fails and is rendered of no value, for it is on the basis of His blood that He makes intercession for His people.

    s.   Hebrews 10:14: "For by one offering he hath perfected for ever them that are sanctified."

The point of this verse is simply that Christ's sacrifice assures every child of God, when saved, of reaching perfection. So valuable is His sacrifice, and so sure our salvation, that the Word speaks as though we are already perfected.

    t.   1 Peter 1:5: "Who are kept by the power of God through faith unto salvation ready to be revealed in the last time."

This verse not only speaks plainly of preservation ("Who are kept by the power of God"), but it shows again that preservation and the assurance of preservation in no way detract from or take away the calling to believe and to do the works of a living faith. Those who are kept are kept through a living faith, and that is the only way they can or will be kept.

    u.   1 Peter 1:23: "Being born again, not of corruptible seed, but of incorruptible, by the word of God, which liveth and abideth for ever."

Peter speaks in this important verse of regeneration and tells us that the incorruptible seed by which we are born again, whatever that may be, is incorruptible and abides forever. In fact, that living seed planted in us and by which we are born again is Christ Himself, Christ in us, the hope of glory (Col. 1:27).

2. Passages that speak of perseverance

Many of the passages at which we have already looked show
the connection between God's preservation and our persevering and make it very clear that God does not preserve His people without also giving them grace and strength to persevere in
holiness and obedience. These are not the only passages, however, that emphasize our calling to persevere. Since the doctrine
is usually called the perseverance of the saints, it is good that
those passages be added to ones we have already cited.

> a. Genesis 18:19: "For I know him, that he will com-
>   mand his children and his household after him, and
>   they shall keep the way of the LORD, to do justice
>   and judgment; that the LORD may bring upon
>   Abraham that which he hath spoken of him."

Here God speaks of Abraham's obedience as the way in which
He will fulfill the promises He made to Abraham. Thus God
speaks also of the certainty of Abraham's continuing in obedience.

> b. Psalm 119:33: "Teach me, O LORD, the way of thy
>   statutes; and I shall keep it unto the end."

Not only does David express in this verse his confidence that
he will persevere in the keeping of God's law until the end, but
he also ascribes this to the grace of God that teaches him the
commandments. We have here, therefore, a beautiful illustration of the teaching that perseverance is by the grace of God
and not by works, yet results in a life of good works.

> c. 1 John 3:2, 3: "Beloved, now are we the sons of
>   God, and it doth not yet appear what we shall be:

but we know that, when he shall appear, we shall be like him; for we shall see him as he is. And every man that hath this hope in him purifieth himself, even as he is pure."

No other text in the Scriptures speaks so plainly, on the one hand, of the fact that once we are made sons of God, we have the certain assurance that we shall someday be like Christ and see Him as He is; and on the other hand, of the fact that this hope does not beget carelessness and carnality but rather holiness and purity.

> d. 1 John 5:18: "We know that whosoever is born of God sinneth not; but he that is begotten of God keepeth himself, and that wicked one toucheth him not."

John says that the devil can no longer overcome those who are regenerated, and the regenerated cannot commit the "unpardonable sin." That is the sin about which John is talking here, as is clear from verses 16 and 17, though he calls it "the sin unto death." Certainly if the regenerated child of God cannot commit the sin unto death, he cannot fall away from God. Nevertheless, he is not careless but keeps himself, even though the whole world lies in wickedness.

The many commands in the Scriptures to continue and persevere, to be holy and continue in holiness, do not imply that the child of God, redeemed by the blood of Christ and regenerated by the Holy Spirit, can fall away from grace and salvation and go lost. They only imply that he can fall, even fall very grievously. Nor do they imply that the doctrine of perseverance encourages careless, immoral, unholy living by Christians. In fact, these many commands, instead of implying that a man can fall away and be lost, or can be and remain a "carnal Christian," are the reason a man may not and cannot continue in sin. He may not, because God forbids it. He cannot, for God uses such commands as these to keep him from falling away and from becoming careless.

D. Difficult passages

A number of Scripture passages are often cited as if they contradict the doctrine of the perseverance of the saints. Before we look at them individually, several comments need to be made that apply to them all.

First, it cannot be denied that these passages do speak of persons "falling away" and perishing, even of their faith being "overthrown."

Second, it cannot be that the Word of God contradicts itself. Either the Word teaches perseverance, or it does not. We do well at this point to remember that the mere preponderance of passages that speak of God's faithfulness and of the power of Christ and of the Holy Spirit as the guarantees of continued and eternal salvation would indicate that the Scriptures *do* teach the perseverance of the saints. The passages that might seem to contradict this are only a few.

Third, all these passages that teach a "falling away of saints" can be answered by one passage of Scripture, 1 John 2:19: "They went out from us, but they were not of us; for if they had been of us, they would no doubt have continued with us: but they went out, that they might be made manifest that they were not all of us."

1 John 2:19 clearly teaches that those who fall away were never really part of the body of believers or of the faith, though it may have appeared for a time that they were. The very fact that they fall away, if indeed they fall away finally and forever, is proof that they never had a part or place in the kingdom of heaven and were never partakers of the saving grace of God in Christ Jesus. They never were elect, never

were purchased by the blood, never received the Holy Spirit and regeneration, never were justified or sanctified, and never had the gift of holiness. They were the stony and thorny soil and the wayside in the parable of Jesus, and the Word, however it affected them, never had root or fruit.

With that in mind, we can easily reconcile with the doctrine of perseverance those passages quoted against it.

1. 1 Samuel 10:6: "And the spirit of the LORD will come upon thee, and thou shalt prophesy with them, and shalt be turned into another man."

This verse speaks of King Saul's receiving the Holy Spirit and even says he would prophesy and be turned into another man. This is sometimes used to contradict the perseverance of saints in light of the rest of the sad story of Saul, which shows him becoming more and more wicked and finally dying in his sins. We should, however, remember several things about Saul:

a. The Holy Spirit as the Spirit of prophecy was sometimes given to those who were not saved. The best examples are Balaam and Caiaphas. Thus, the fact that Saul prophesied does not prove him to be a child of God.

b. The Holy Spirit gives other gifts besides the blessings of salvation, and He certainly did give Saul the gift of courage and zeal, both of which were necessary for his work as king (1 Sam. 11:6). This is very likely all that Samuel meant when he said that Saul would become another man, since Saul was originally too fearful and cowardly to assume the duties of the kingdom (1 Sam. 10:21, 22).

c. There is no indication in the Scriptures that Saul had any of the marks of regeneration. He never showed any signs of true repentance, even in the beginning, nor any zeal for God.

d. In fact, the testimony of the Scriptures leads us in the opposite direction and seems to indicate that Saul was not only an unregenerated person but was known as such in Israel, so that his prophesying became a byword among the people for anything done out of character (1 Sam. 10:11, 12).

2. Galatians 5:4: "Christ is become of no effect unto you, whosoever of you are justified by the law; ye are fallen from grace."

Here is a verse that actually uses the words "fallen from grace." Paul is speaking to those who wanted to make circumcision a condition for salvation and for membership in the Christian church, and he tells them that if this is what they believe, then not only is Christ become of no effect to them, but they are fallen from grace.

The correct explanation is very simple. Paul is not saying that these people once received the grace of God and have now lost it and are perishing, but that they, by their belief in salvation through law-works, have separated themselves from salvation by grace and from the cross of Christ. They stand by their own teaching as those for whom the cross is of "none effect" and to whom grace is meaningless.

3. 2 Timothy 2:18: "Who concerning the truth have erred, saying that the resurrection is past already; and overthrow the faith of some."

Paul refers to the faith of some being "overthrown" by the false teaching of Hymanaeus and Philetus in 2 Timothy 2:18. Two things must be remembered here:

a. In the very next verse the Word of God assures us that the Lord knows them that are His, implying that the faith of those who are His cannot be overthrown.

b. The Scriptures do speak of a faith that is not a true and saving faith (Matt. 13:19–21; James 2:14–20). It is the only kind of faith that can be overthrown, for true faith is a gift and work of God. Those, then, of whom the Scriptures are speaking in this verse are those who never had true faith, whom the Lord never knew, who were never of the company of true believers, and who never departed from iniquity. They were hypocrites.

4. Hebrews 6:4–6: "For it is impossible for those who were once enlightened, and have tasted of the heavenly gift, and were made partakers of the Holy Ghost, And have tasted the good word of God, and the powers of the world to come. If they shall fall away, to renew them again unto repentance; seeing they crucify to themselves the Son of God afresh, and put him to an open shame."

No passage is used so often as this to teach a falling away of saints, since it speaks of those who were enlightened, tasted of the heavenly gift, were made partakers of the Holy Spirit, tasted the good Word of God and the powers of the world to come, and who yet fell away and cannot be renewed to repentance.

We must remember that the Holy Spirit gives other gifts and does other works than salvation, and that it is not impossible for an unbelieving person to see, at least intellectually and emotionally, the blessedness of salvation to the extent that he feigns faith and obedience (Matt. 13:19–21; Acts 8:9–23;

Acts 26:28). Also, it may not be forgotten that this passage, rather than teaching that it is possible to be saved over and over again, teaches instead the impossibility of renewing to repentance the people described. Finally, if this passage does indeed teach a falling away of saints, it contradicts the context, for in verses 9–19 the chapter teaches the perseverance of saints, founding the hope of perseverance on the immutability of God's own counsel and oath.

We must conclude, therefore, that the text speaks of those who come under the gospel and its call, are taught the Scriptures, hear the promises, and perhaps even respond emotionally to the gospel, but who are nevertheless spiritually dead and never bear true fruit. They are like the barren earth of which Hebrews 6:8 speaks. Rather than teaching a falling away of saints, the passage, then, speaks of the terrible judgment that shall come on all those who hear the gospel and turn from it, and of their greater damnation. It stands as a warning to all hearers of the Word.

> 5. Hebrews 10:26, 27: "For if we sin wilfully after that we have received the knowledge of the truth, there remaineth no more sacrifice for sins, But a certain fearful looking for of judgment and fiery indignation, which shall devour the adversaries."

Many interpret these verses as though they teach that it is possible for sacrifice to be made once for a person's sins and then for that person through unbelief to lose salvation and come under the judgment of God.

This is not what the text says, however. We should note that the passage very carefully speaks of "those who have received the *knowledge* of the truth" and does not say that sacrifice for sin was made for them. In fact, the word "more" in the King James version leaves an entirely wrong impression. The idea is not that there is no *additional* sacrifice for sin (over and above what they have already received) but that there is *no longer* any possibility of sacrifice for sin for them. In other words, the passage is talking about those who commit what is sometimes known as the "unforgiveable sin," that is, those who with full knowledge of the truth willfully reject it, and by that show themselves beyond any hope of salvation.

6. 2 Peter 2:1: "But there were false prophets also among the people, even as there shall be false teachers among you, who privily shall bring in damnable heresies, even denying the Lord that bought them, and bring upon themselves swift destruction."

At first glance this verse might be taken as contradicting the perseverance of the saints. It is, in fact, sometimes quoted as though it says that some deny the Lord who bought them. The passage then would be speaking of those who had been purchased by the blood of Christ and who perhaps had even been brought to believe that, but now deny it to their own condemnation and destruction.

The text really says the opposite about these people. It not only calls them false teachers, but it says that they brought in with them, that is, into the church, their damnable heresies. Nor is the idea of the passage that Christ bought them and now they deny Him, but that their damnable heresy, brought with them into the church, is a denial of the blood of atonement that was shed as the only way of salvation. The passage, therefore, does not contradict the rest of the Scriptures and really does not speak to the matter of perseverance at all! It only condemns any denial of the atonement as a damnable heresy.

E. Objection

The chief objection brought against the doctrine of perseverance is that it leads to carelessness on the part of Christians,
so that they are not as concerned about holiness and Christian living as they should be.

Against this objection stand all the passages cited above
that show that the doctrine of perseverance is in no sense of
the word a denial of our responsibility to be godly and holy
in all our conduct and speech, and even in our thoughts and
motives.

It is interesting, though, that the Bible itself deals with this
objection in several places. Both in Romans 3:5–8 and in Romans 6:1, 2 Paul deals with the idea that grace encourages
sinning. That, of course, is a step beyond the idea that sovereign grace leaves a person without any reason to be holy. In
this case, some were apparently saying that the doctrines of
grace (including perseverance) were themselves a reason for
sinning, since the more a person sins, the more God's grace is
revealed.

The Bible deals very harshly with this idea and with those
who taught it. Paul says in Romans 3:8 that those who say
such things speak slander and will suffer damnation. His answer in Romans 6:2 is by itself a sufficient answer to all who
might think this: "God forbid. How shall we, that are dead to
sin, live any longer therein?"

In Romans 6 Paul goes on to explain what is really the answer of the Scriptures to all such objections, that is, that grace
is *one*. The same grace by which we are chosen, redeemed, and
preserved also leads us inevitably to holiness by bringing us
regeneration, sanctification, calling, and conversion. No one
can have just *part* of grace. He cannot possibly be chosen and
justified without also being sanctified and made holy. If he has
no holiness, the only possible explanation is that he is not cho-

sen or redeemed, either. There cannot possibly be such a thing as a "carnal Christian."

F. Denials of the perseverance of the saints
1. Roman Catholicism

On the one hand, the Roman Catholic Church teaches that the grace of justification can be lost, and not just the assurance of justification. This, according to Roman Catholic teaching, is true to the extent that a man who has lost that grace must be justified all over again. In fact, one loses one's justification every time one commits a mortal sin, and one is rejustified through the sacrament of penance. This, of course, goes along with the Roman Catholic teaching of salvation by good works. If salvation is by works, then to cease from works is to lose salvation. Hence, Rome's conclusion regarding perseverance is that although there is hope for it, there is no absolute certainty of it. This clearly contradicts the teaching of Scripture, which founds the certainty of perseverance not on our faithfulness and good works, but on the grace and sovereignty of God.

On the other hand, however, the Roman Catholic Church encourages a false security by teaching a kind of automatic salvation merely through the receiving of the sacraments from the church. This is really a denial of the *perseverance* of saints, since it encourages carelessness and wickedness and discourages the daily battle against sin.

2. Arminianism

Arminianism, the false teaching against which the Five Points of Calvinism were originally formulated, teaches and has always taught that it is possible to be redeemed in Christ and regenerated by the Spirit and yet lose everything and perish everlastingly. Along with this, Arminianism teaches that it is possible not only for believers to commit the sin unto death, but also for those who have fallen away to be regenerated again and again.

This not only contradicts the passages that clearly teach the perseverance of saints, but even the passage that is most often used to defend a falling away of saints, Hebrews 6:1–4, which states that there is *no* renewing to repentance for those who do fall away. But let us not forget that this denial of perseverance always accompanies a denial of unconditional election. If election is indeed unconditional, then it guarantees perseverance. If it depends on man's works or faith, then perseverance depends on man's works also and is not guaranteed.

Thus, the difference between Arminianism and Calvinism is not just that one denies and the other accepts the doctrine of perseverance, but that they each have a different understanding of what a saint is. Arminianism views a saint as one who is such by his own faith and free will, while Calvinism looks at the saint as someone made such by God. This, of course, makes all the difference, for if we are saints by our own faith and obedience, then our continuing as saints also depends on our faithfulness and choice. If we are saints by the grace of God, then our persevering depends upon sure, faithful, infallible grace alone.

1 Peter 1:23 is especially important here, because it shows that regeneration, the very first work of God's grace in us, is something that takes place through the planting of an *incorruptible* and *ever-abiding* seed.

3. Free will

This teaching that man has of himself a free will to choose God and salvation, and that faith is an act of man's own will, is really just a form of Arminianism. Obviously, it has no room for any doctrine of perseverance, since if the faith by which we are saved is indeed an act of our own will, then whether or not we retain that faith also depends on our will, which can and does change. Only if salvation depends on God's will, and not on man's, can there be any security and hope of perseverance for saints.

4. Antinomianism

This error is on the opposite end of the spectrum from Arminianism. It teaches that because God preserves His people, because election is sure, and because the blood of the cross is efficacious, there is no urgency in the call to holiness and good works and that it is possible that a Christian, chosen and redeemed, continues carnal and unholy. It suggests that a Christian need not and even cannot do the good work of prayer and worshiping God and that it is a repudiation of the doctrines of sovereign grace and perseverance to read and preach the law of God and to call men to repentance, faith, holiness, and perseverance.

The misunderstanding that leads to these errors is easily seen. It is this: that the call to repentance, faith, and holiness implies that sinners in and of themselves have the ability to heed that call, whether it be the call to faith or the call to persevere in the faith. That is not true, for the call of the gospel is powerful only to those who receive the Spirit, and it is heard by the rest to their condemnation, not at all implying that they are able to heed it.

Even more important is the fact that the Scriptures flatly contradict this error. The Bible in teaching doctrines of sovereign grace, neither encourages or allows for sin and carelessness (Rom. 6:1, 2). The doctrine of perseverance does not do so, either. 1 John 3:3 says, "Every man that hath this hope in him [of persevering to the end and seeing Christ] purifieth himself, even as he is pure."

5. The "carnal Christian" teaching

A modern form of antinomianism is the teaching that there is such a thing as a "carnal Christian." This notion arises out of Arminian evangelism and the theology of salvation by "accepting Jesus." In the interest of preserving the appearance of success, which this kind of evangelism with its large number of conversions seems to have, this new class of Christians has been invented. The invention is necessary because such evangelism, more often than not, results neither in godliness nor in faithful church membership. To deny that such people were ever actually converted would be to deny its supposed success.

Hebrews 12:14 is clear. Without holiness no man shall see the Lord.

6. The denial of "Lordship" salvation

Closely associated with the "carnal Christian" teaching is a denial of Lordship salvation. Some say, wrongly, that a person can have Jesus as Savior without having Him as Lord. In other words, a person can be saved, but without having Jesus as the Lord of His life. A person in whose life Jesus does not rule is, according to such teaching, a person who continues to live the same kind of life he or she did before being saved, a life that shows no fruits of faith, but is still carnal and worldly.

How a person could possibly have Jesus as Savior and not as Lord is impossible to understand, for it is as a sovereign and gracious Lord that He saves us and makes us His own. In saving us He substitutes His rule for that of sin and Satan and translates us from the kingdom of darkness to His own kingdom. He does not leave us with no Lord, as that would be leaving us to perish, but makes Himself our blessed and only Potentate.

7. Perfectionism

Perfectionism goes to the opposite extreme and denies entirely the need for God's preserving grace and for our persevering by that grace. It teaches that it is possible, desirable, and even normal for a Christian to live a life that is free from sin, or from all known sin. Obviously, if the Christian has reached such a state of perfection, there is no sense in talking about his being preserved or persevering.

Pentecostalism teaches this as does the pernicious idea of a "victorious Christian life." So does the "health and wealth" gospel, though from a little different viewpoint. The "health and wealth" gospel teaches that there is no need for perseverance, because the Christian in this life is to be free from sickness, poverty, suffering, and trial. The "positive thinking" enthusiasts, and all such who teach that the solution to life's problems is mental or psychological, also deny any need for perseverance.

Not only is this all nonsense, contrary to the experience of believers; not only does it destroy their peace when troubles and temptations do come; but it is also against the Word of God, which tells us in 1 Peter 4:18 that the righteous are scarcely saved, and which assures us in Romans 8:17 that only if we suffer with Christ will we be glorified with Him. There are simply too many passages that speak of temptations and trials for these lies to be true. They are flatly contradicted by the complaint of the apostle Paul in Romans 7:19: "For the good that I would [thus showing that he speaks as a regenerated child of God] I do not: but the evil which I would not [thus also showing his regeneration, for no unregenerated person can will the good or hate evil as Paul does here], that I do."

G. Practical importance

The doctrine of perseverance is a most valuable treasure of the church and of the people of God, not only because it so powerfully demonstrates the sovereignty of God in all of salvation, but also because it is full of practical implications.

1. Perseverance and prayer

Because Calvinism teaches so strongly that preservation and perseverence are two sides of the same coin, the doctrine of perseverance is another way of stressing the importance of prayer in the Christian life. According to Calvinism and Scripture, there is no hope of perseverance without prayer, for it is through prayer that we receive grace to persevere.

This is the teaching of the Canons of Dordt in Chapter V, Article 4: "Although the weakness of the flesh cannot prevail against the power of God, who confirms and preserves true believers in a state of grace, yet converts are not always so influenced and actuated by the Spirit of God, as not in some particular instances sinfully to deviate from the guidance of divine grace, so as to be seduced by, and comply with the lusts of the flesh; they must, therefore, be constant in watching and prayer, that they be not led into temptation. When these are neglected, they are not only liable to be drawn into great and heinous sins by Satan, the world and the flesh, but sometimes by the righteous permission of God actually fall into these evils. This, the lamentable fall of David, Peter, and other saints described in Holy Scripture, demonstrates."

Scripture confirms this in many places, notably in Matthew 26:41: "Watch and pray, that ye enter not into temptation: the spirit indeed is willing, but the flesh is weak."

2. Perseverance and the preaching of the gospel

What is true of prayer is also true of preaching. It is the other great means God uses to preserve and keep His people. The warnings, admonitions, and encouragements of His Word are designed exactly for that purpose. This means, then, that the doctrine of perseverance, rightly understood, magnifies the importance of the preaching of the gospel and its necessity in the lives of believers. Rather than destroying lively gospel preaching, the doctrines of grace make it necessary and give power to it, for grace is through the preaching.

That perseverance requires gospel preaching is clear from John 10:27, 28: "My sheep *hear my voice,* and I know them, and they follow me: And I give unto them eternal life; and they shall never perish, neither shall any man pluck them out of my hand." Only through the preaching of the gospel do we hear the voice of Jesus. That is our hope of never perishing.

3. Perseverance and holiness

Again the calumnies of those who hate Calvinism are shown false. The doctrines of grace do not destroy holiness and promote carelessness and worldliness, as some have charged. Rather, the call to perseverance *is* the call to holiness, and it makes no sense even to talk about perseverance except in terms of holiness, godliness, Christian piety, and faithful obedience.

We believe that God surely and infallibly preserves His people, but only in the way of their persevering in holiness, so that without holiness no one shall see the Lord (Heb. 12:14).

4. Perseverance and peace

It should also be evident that only the doctrine of perseverance can give Christians any peace in the world. In view of the fact that they fight against principalities and powers and spiritual wickedness, and in view of the fact that they themselves are sinful and weak, they know that there is no hope of glory for them apart from the grace of God. The doctrine of perseverance assures them that God is faithful and that He will not abandon or turn away from the work He has begun in them, though they themselves may feel that that work is very small.

A good example of this is to be found in the questioning of persons who are struggling to find assurance of salvation. The very fact that they are concerned and afraid is the fruit of God's saving grace working in them, and they can and must be told that God Himself will continue that work of grace and bring it to full fruit.

In persecution, in suffering, and in temptation, each one of God's people, through the doctrine of perseverance, may rest on the faithfulness and grace of God and know that nothing can separate him from God and eternal life. Believing in the doctrine of the perseverance of the saints, one believes in God Himself, in His love and mercy and grace and unchangeableness, and finds in them hope and peace.

H. Relation to the other four points

In conclusion let us remember that the doctrine of perseverance is inseparably connected with the other Five Points of Calvinism. The elect are preserved, but they are preserved because God has chosen them and because Christ died for them. They need that preserving grace because in themselves they are totally depraved and can do no good, *certainly* not the great good of finding and obtaining life everlasting. The grace that God gives them is powerful and irresistible, so that not only their own sins, but even the devil and the whole wicked world, cannot prevent them from being saved with an everlasting salvation.

To deny the doctrine of perseverance is to say that God's counsel can be changed, that God Himself can change. It is to say that Christ groaned and bled and died on Calvary for nothing, that God's promise can fail, and that the gifts and calling of God can be revoked, and that by weak, sinful man himself. God forbid that it should be so. Thanks be to Him for the work of grace, sovereignly begun, sovereignly brought forward, and sovereignly finished.

Soli Deo Gloria!

Notes

Chapter I

1. John Calvin, "The Eternal Predestination of God," in *Calvin's Calvinism: Treatises on "The Eternal Predestination of God" and "The Secret Providence of God,"* trans. Henry Cole (Grand Rapids, Mich.: Reformed Free Publishing Association, [1987]), 43.

2. John Calvin, *Institutes of the Christian Religion,* ed. by John T. McNeill, tr. by Ford Lewis Battles in vol. 1 of 2 vols., found in volume XX of the Library of Christian Classics (Philadelphia: The Westminster Press, 1960), Bk. I, chap. 1, sect. 1, 35.

3. Ibid, Bk. 1, chap. 1, sect. 2, 37.

Chapter III

1. Calvin, "The Eternal Predestination of God," 31.

Chapter IV

1. We refer our readers to A. W. Pink's *The Sovereignty of God* and to the pamphlet by Homer C. Hoeksema entitled "God So Loved the World," both given in the Recommended Reading section (Appendix I).

Chapter V

1. E. Gordon Rupp, ed. *Luther and Erasmus: Free Will and Salvation,* in The Library of Christian Classics, vol. 17 (Philadelphia: The Westminster Press, 1969), 47.

2. Quoted in Homer C. Hoeksema, *The Voice of Our Fathers* (Grand Rapids, Mich.: Reformed Free Publishing Association, 1980), 106.

Appendix III

1. Quotations from the creeds are taken from the following sources: "The Three Forms of Unity: Heidelberg Catechism, Belgic Confession, Canons of Dordt" (Grand Rapids, Mich.: Mission Committee of the Protestant Reformed Churches in America, 1983); and *The Confession of Faith; the Larger and Shorter Catechisms, with the Scripture Proofs at Large: together with the Sum of Saving Knowledge,* etc. (Glasgow: Free Presbyterian Publications, 1985).

Recommended Reading

The following list of books is recommended to those who might be interested in further study of the doctrines of grace. The list is not intended to be exhaustive but is nevertheless fairly comprehensive. Some of the books are currently in print; others are not. Recommendation of a book is not to be understood as endorsement of every idea set forth by its author. Especially recommended are the books marked with an asterisk.

Boettner, Loraine. *The Reformed Doctrine of Predestination.* Philadelphia: Presbyterian and Reformed Publishing Co., 1978.

Buis, Harry. *Historic Protestantism and Predestination.* Philadelphia: Presbyterian and Reformed Publishing Co., 1958.

*Calvin, John. *Calvin's Calvinism: Treatises on "The Eternal Predestination of God" and "The Secret Providence of God."* Tr. by Henry Cole. Grand Rapids, Mich.: Reformed Free Publishing Association, [1987].

Clark, Gordon H. *Biblical Predestination.* Phillipsburg, N.J.: Presbyterian and Reformed Publishing Co., 1969.

*Coles, Elisha. *God's Sovereignty.* Grand Rapids, Mich.: Baker Book House, 1979.

Coppes, Leonard H. *Are Five Points Enough? The Ten Points of Calvinism.* Manassas, Va.: Reformation Educational Foundation, 1980.

Dabney, Robert L. *The Five Points of Calvinism.* Harrisonburg, Va.: Sprinkle Publications, 1992.

Dakin, A. *Calvinism*. Philadelphia: The Westminster Press, 1946.

*Engelsma, David J. *Hyper-Calvinism and the Call of the Gospel: An Examination of the "Well-Meant Offer" of the Gospel.* Rev. 2nd Ed. Grand Rapids, Mich.: Reformed Free Publishing Association, 1994.

*Gill, John. *The Cause of God and Truth*. Paris, Arkansas: Baptist Standard Press, 1992.

Girardeau, John L. *Calvinism and Evangelical Arminianism Compared as to Election, Reprobation, Justification, and Related Doctrines.* Harrisonburg, Va.: Sprinkle Publications, 1984.

Hoeksema, Homer C., "God So Loved the World . . ." South Holland, Ill.: Evangelism Committee, South Holland Protestant Reformed Church, 1994.

Hoeksema, Homer C., *The Voice of Our Fathers* [an exposition of the Canons of Dordrecht]. Grand Rapids, Mich.: Reformed Free Publishing Association, 1980.

*Hanko, Herman, Homer C. Hoeksema, and Gise J. Van Baren. *The Five Points of Calvinism*. Grand Rapids, Mich.: Reformed Free Publishing Association, 1976.

Luther, Martin. *The Bondage of the Will*. Tr. by J. I. Packer and O. R. Johnston. Westwood, N.J.: Fleming H. Revell Co., 1957.

McNeill, John T. *The History and Character of Calvinism*. London: Oxford University Press, 1973.

Ness, Christopher. *An Antidote to Arminianism*. North Hollywood, Calif: Puritan Heritage Publications, 1978.

Palmer, Edwin H. *The Five Points of Calvinism*. Grand Rapids, Mich.: Baker Book House, 1972.

*Parks, William. *Sermons on the Five Points of Calvinism*. London: Sovereign Grace Union, 1929.

*Pink, Arthur W. *The Sovereignty of God*. Grand Rapids, Mich.: Baker Book House, 1963.

Shedd, William G. T. *Calvinism, Pure and Mixed*. Edinburgh: Banner of Truth, 1986.

Spencer, Duane Edward. *TULIP: The Five Points of Calvinism in the Light of Scripture.* Grand Rapids, Mich.: Baker Book House, 1979.

*Sproul, R. C. *Chosen by God*. Wheaton, Ill.: Tyndale House Publishers Inc., 1986.

*Steele, David N. and Curtis C. Thomas. *The Five Points of Calvinism: Defined, Defended, Documented*. Philadelphia: Presbyterian and Reformed Publishing Co., 1963.

Thornwell, James Henly. *Election and Reprobation*. Jackson, Miss.: Presbyterian Reformation Society, 1961.

Warburton, Ben A. *Calvinism: Its History and Basic Principles, Its Fruits and Its Future, and Its Practical Application to Life*. Grand Rapids, Mich.: Wm. B. Eerdmans Publishing Co., 1955.

Zanchius, Jerome. *The Doctrine of Absolute Predestination*. Tr. by Augustus M. Toplady. Grand Rapids, Mich.: Baker Book House, 1977.

Arminianism and Calvinism Compared

Arminianism (the Five F's)	Calvinism (TULIP)
1. Free will	1. T-otal depravity
2. Foreseen faith	2. U-nconditional election
3. For everyone	3. L-imited atonement
4. Final decision with man	4. I-rresistible grace
5. Falling away	5. P-erseverance of the saints

APPENDIX III

Citations from the Creeds

Since the doctrines covered by the Five Points of Calvinism are expressed in a very concise way in the creeds of the church, especially in the Reformed and Presbyterian creeds, it is helpful, in trying to understand the doctrines, to make reference to some of these statements. Most of the quotations given below are from the Heidelberg Catechism, the Belgic Confession, and the Canons of Dordrecht (Dordt), the three major creeds of those churches that have the name Reformed; the rest of the quotations are from the Westminster Confession of Faith and the Westminster Larger Catechism, which are from the Presbyterian tradition. Since the Canons of Dordt are the original Five Points of Calvinism, their statements concerning the Five Points are of special significance. As in chapters 1–6, certain words have been italicized to draw the reader's attention to key portions that illustrate the point being made. Some of the quotations represent only a part of the given question and answer, or article. See Notes directly following chapter 6 for sources used.[1]

A. THE SOVEREIGNTY OF GOD
   1. HEIDELBERG CATECHISM
      a. Lord's Day 9
      Question and Answer 26
      Q. What believest thou when thou sayest, "I believe in God the Father, *Almighty,* Maker of heaven and earth"?

A. That the eternal Father of our Lord Jesus Christ (who of nothing made heaven and earth, with all that is in them; who likewise upholds and governs the same by his eternal counsel and providence) is for the sake of Christ his Son, my God and my Father; on whom I rely so entirely, that I have no doubt, but he will provide me with all things necessary for soul and body; and further, that he will make whatever evils he sends upon me, in this valley of tears turn out to my advantage; *for he is able to do it, being Almighty God,* and willing, being a faithful Father.

(Scripture proofs: Gen. 1; Gen. 2; Ps. 33:6; Ps. 115:3; Matt. 10:29; Heb. 1:3; John 5:17; John 1:12, 16; Rom. 8:15, 16; Gal. 4:5, 6; Eph. 1:5; 1 John 3:1; Ps. 55:22; Matt. 6:26; Rom. 8:28; Rom. 4:21; Rom. 10:12; Matt. 6:26; Matt. 7:9–11.)

b. Lord's Day 10

Question and Answer 27

Q. What dost thou mean by the providence of God?

A. *The almighty and everywhere present power of God;* whereby, as it were by his hand, he upholds and governs heaven, earth, and all creatures; so that herbs and grass, rain and drought, fruitful and barren years, meat and drink, health and sickness, riches and poverty, yea, and *all things come, not by chance, but by his fatherly hand.*

(Scripture proofs: Acts 17:25–28; Heb. 1:3; Jer. 5:24; Acts 14:17; John 9:3; Prov. 22:2; Job 1:21; Matt. 10:29, 30; Eph. 1:11.)

c. Lord's Day 10

Question and Answer 28

Q. What advantage is it to us to know that God has created, and by his providence doth still uphold all things?

A. That we may be patient in adversity; thankful in prosperity; and that in all things, which may hereafter befall us, we place our firm trust in our faithful God and Father, that nothing shall separate us from his love; since *all creatures are so in his hand, that without his will they cannot so much as move.*

(Scripture proofs: Rom. 5:3; Ps. 39:10; Deut. 8:10; 1 Thess. 5:18; Rom. 5:3–6; Rom. 8:38, 39; Job 1:12; Job 2:6; Matt. 8:31; Isa. 10:15.)

d. Lord's Day 19

Question and Answer 50

Q. Why is it added, "and sitteth at the right hand of God"?

A. Because Christ is ascended into heaven for this end, that he might appear as head of his church, by whom *the Father governs all things.*

(Scripture proofs: Eph. 1:20–22; Col. 1:18; Matt. 28:18; John 5:22.)

e. Lord's Day 19

Question and Answer 51

Q. What profit is this glory of Christ, our head, unto us?

A. First, that by his Holy Spirit he pours out heavenly graces upon us his members; and then that *by his power he defends and preserves us against all enemies.*

(Scripture proofs: Eph. 4:8; Ps. 2:9; John 10:28.)

f. Lord's Day 52

Question and Answer 128

Q. How dost thou conclude thy prayer?

A. "For thine is the kingdom, and the power, and the glory, for ever"; that is, all these we ask of thee, because thou, being our King and *almighty,* art willing and able to give us all good; and all this we pray for, that thereby not we, but thy holy name, may be glorified for ever.

(Scripture proofs: Matt. 6:13; Rom. 10:12; 2 Pet. 2:9; John 14:13; Ps. 115:1; Phil. 4:20.)

2. (BELGIC) CONFESSION OF FAITH

a. Article 12

We believe that the Father, by the Word, that is, by his Son, hath created of nothing, the heaven, the earth, and all creatures, *as it seemed good unto him,* giving unto every creature its being, shape, form, and several offices to serve its Creator. That he doth also still uphold and govern them by his eternal providence, and *infinite power,* for the service of mankind, to the end that man may serve his God.

b. Article 13

We believe that the same God, after he had created all things, did not forsake them, or give them up to fortune or chance, but that he *rules and governs them according to his holy will, so that nothing happens in this world without his appointment:* nevertheless, God neither is the author of, nor can be charged with, the sins which are committed. For *his power and goodness are so great and incomprehensible, that he orders and executes his work in the most excellent and just manner, even then, when devils and wicked men act unjustly.* And, as to what he doth surpassing human understanding, we will not curiously inquire into, farther than our capacity will admit of; but with the greatest humility and reverence adore the righteous judgments of God, which are hid from us, contenting ourselves that we are disciples of Christ, to learn only those things which he has revealed to us in his Word, without transgressing these limits. This doctrine affords us unspeakable consolation, since we are taught thereby that nothing can befall us by chance, but by the direction of our most gracious and heavenly Father; who watches over us with a paternal care, *keeping all creatures so under his power, that not a hair of our head (for they are all numbered), nor a sparrow, can fall to the ground, without the will of our Father,* in whom we do entirely trust; being persuaded, that he so restrains the devil and all our enemies, that without his will and permission, they cannot hurt us. And therefore we reject that damnable error of the Epicureans, who say that God regards nothing, but leaves all things to chance.

3. CANONS OF DORDT

a. First Head of Doctrine, Article 7

Election is the unchangeable purpose of God, whereby, before the foundation of the world, he hath out of mere grace, according to the *sovereign good pleasure of his own will,* chosen, from the whole human race, which had fallen through their own fault, from their primitive state of rectitude, into sin and destruction, a certain number of persons to redemption in Christ, whom he from eternity appointed the Mediator and Head of the elect, and the foundation of salvation.

This elect number, though by nature neither better nor more deserving than others, but with them involved in one common misery, God hath decreed to give to Christ, to be saved by him, and effectually to call and draw them to his communion by his Word and Spirit, to bestow upon them true faith, justification and sanctification; and having powerfully preserved them in the fellowship of his Son, finally, to glorify them for the demonstration of his mercy, and for the praise of his glorious grace; as it is written: "According as he hath chosen us in him, before the foundation of the world, that we should be holy, and without blame before him in love; having predestinated us unto the adoption of children by Jesus Christ to himself, according to the good pleasure of his will, to the praise of the glory of his grace, wherein he hath made us accepted in the beloved" (Eph. 1:4–6). And elsewhere: "Whom he did predestinate, them he also called, and whom he called, them he also justified, and whom he justified them he also glorified" (Rom. 8:30).

b. First Head of Doctrine, Article 11

And as God himself is most wise, unchangeable, omniscient and *omnipotent,* so the election made by him can neither be interrupted nor changed, recalled or annulled; neither can the elect be cast away, nor their number diminished.

c. First Head of Doctrine, Article 15

What peculiarly tends to illustrate and recommend to us the eternal and unmerited grace of election, is the express testimony of sacred Scripture, that not all, but some only are elected, while others are passed by in the eternal decree; whom *God, out of his sovereign, most just, irreprehensible and unchangeable good pleasure,* hath decreed to leave in the common misery into which they have wilfully plunged themselves, and not to bestow upon them saving faith and the grace of conversion; but permitting them in his just judgment to follow their own ways, at last for the declaration of his justice, to condemn and perish them forever, not only on account of their unbelief, but also for all their other sins. And this is the decree of reprobation which by no means makes God the author of sin (the very thought of which is blasphemy), but declares him to be an awful, irreprehensible, and righteous judge and avenger thereof.

d. Second Head of Doctrine, Article 8

For this was the *sovereign counsel,* and most gracious will and purpose of God the Father, that the quickening and saving efficacy of the most precious death of his Son should extend to all the elect, for bestowing upon them alone the gift of justifying faith, thereby to bring them infallibly to salvation: that is, it was the will of God, that Christ by the blood of the cross, whereby he confirmed the new covenant, should effectually redeem out of every people, tribe, nation, and language, all those, and those only, who were from eternity chosen to salvation, and given to him by the Father; that he should confer upon them faith, which together with all the other saving gifts of the Holy Spirit, he purchased for them by his death; should purge them from all sin, both original and actual, whether committed before or after believing; and having faithfully preserved them even to the end, should at last bring them free from every spot and blemish to the enjoyment of glory in his own presence forever.

4. WESTMINSTER CONFESSION OF FAITH

a. Chapter 2, Article 2

God hath all life, glory, goodness, blessedness, in and of himself; and is alone in and unto himself all-sufficient, not standing in need of any creatures which he hath made, nor deriving any glory from them, but only manifesting his own glory, in, by, unto, and upon them: he is the alone fountain of all being, of whom, through whom, and to whom, are all things; and hath *most sovereign dominion over them, to do by them, for them, or upon them, whatsoever himself pleaseth.*

(Scripture proofs: John 5:26; Acts 7:2; Ps. 119:68; 1 Tim. 6:15; Rom. 9:5; Acts 17:24, 25; Job 22:2, 3; Rom. 11:36; Rev. 4:11; 1 Tim. 6:15; Dan. 4:25, 35; Heb. 4:13; Rom. 11:33, 34; Ps. 147:5; Acts 15:18; Ezek. 11:5; Ps. 145:17; Rom. 7:12; Rev. 5:12–14.)

b. Chapter 5, Article 1

God, the great Creator of all things, *doth uphold, direct, dispose, and govern all creatures,* actions, and things, from the greatest even to the least, by his most wise and holy providence, according to his infallible foreknowledge, and the free and immutable counsel of his own will, to the praise of the glory of his wisdom, power, justice, goodness, and mercy.

(Scripture proofs: Heb. 1:3; Dan. 4:34, 35; Ps. 135:6; Acts 17:25, 26, 28; Job 38–41; Matt. 10:29–31; Prov. 15:3; Ps. 104:24; Ps. 145:17; Acts 15:18; Ps. 94:8–11; Eph. 1:11; Ps. 33:10, 11; Isa. 63:14; Eph. 3:10; Rom. 9:17; Gen. 45:7; Ps. 145:7.)

c. Chapter 5, Article 4

The *almighty power,* unsearchable wisdom, and infinite goodness of God, so far manifest themselves in his providence, that it extendeth itself even to the first fall, and all other sins of angels and men, and that not by a bare permission, but such as hath joined with it a most wise and *powerful bounding,* and otherwise ordering and governing of them, in a manifold dispensation, to his own holy ends; yet so as the sinfulness thereof proceedeth only from the creature, and not from God; who, being most holy and righteous, neither is nor can be the author or approver of sin.

(Scripture proofs: Rom. 11:32–34; 2 Sam. 24:1; 1 Chron. 21:1; 1 Kings 22:22, 23; 1 Chron. 10:4, 13, 14; 2 Sam. 16:10; Acts 2:23; Acts 4:27, 28; Acts 14:16; Ps. 76:10; 2 Kings 19:28; Gen. 50:20; Isa. 10:6, 7, 12; James 1:13, 14, 17; 1 John 2:16; Ps. 50:21.)

5. WESTMINSTER LARGER CATECHISM
a. *Question and Answer 7*

Q. What is God?

A. God is a Spirit, in and of himself infinite in being, glory, blessedness, and perfection; all-sufficient, eternal, unchangeable, incomprehensible, every where present, *almighty,* knowing all things, most wise, most holy, most just, most merciful and gracious, long-suffering, and abundant in goodness and truth.

(Scripture proofs: John 4:24; Ex. 3:14; Job 11:7–9; Acts 7:2; 1 Tim. 6:15; Matt. 5:48; Gen. 17:1; Ps. 90:2; Mal. 3:6; James 1:17; 1 Kings 8:27; Ps. 139:1–13; Rev. 4:8; Heb. 4:13; Ps. 147:5; Rom. 16:27; Isa. 6:3; Rev. 15:4; Deut. 32:4; Ex. 34:6.)

B. TOTAL DEPRAVITY
1. HEIDELBERG CATECHISM
a. Lord's Day 2

Question and Answer 5

Q. Canst thou keep all these things [of the law] perfectly?

A. In no wise; for I am *prone by nature* to hate God and my neighbor.

(Scripture proofs: Rom. 3:10; 1 John 1:8; Rom. 8:7; Tit. 3:3.)

b. Lord's Day 3

Question and Answer 7

Q. Whence then proceeds this *depravity of human nature?*
A. From the fall and disobedience of our first parents, Adam and Eve, in Paradise; hence *our nature* is become *so corrupt,* that we are *all* conceived and born in sin.

(Scripture proofs: Gen. 3:6; Rom. 5:12, 18, 19; Ps. 51:5; Gen. 5:3.)

c. Lord's Day 3

Question and Answer 8

Q. Are we then so corrupt that we are *wholly incapable of doing any good, and inclined to all wickedness?*
A. Indeed we are; except we are regenerated by the Spirit of God.

(Scripture proofs: Gen. 6:5; Job 14:4; Job 15:14, 16; John 3:5; Eph. 2:5.)

d. Lord's Day 21

Question and Answer 56

Q. What believest thou concerning "the forgiveness of sins"?
A. That God, for the sake of Christ's satisfaction, will no more remember my sins, *neither my corrupt nature,* against which I have to struggle all my life long; but will graciously impute to me the righteousness of Christ, that I may never be condemned before the tribunal of God.

(Scripture proofs: 1 John 2:2; 2 Cor. 5:19, 21; Jer. 31:34; Ps. 103:3, 4, 10, 11; Rom. 8:1–3; John 3:18.)

e. Lord's Day 23

Question and Answer 60

Q. How art thou righteous before God?
A. Only by a true faith in Jesus Christ; so that, though my conscience accuse me, that I have *grossly* transgressed *all* the commandments of God, and *kept none* of them, and am still inclined to *all evil;* notwithstanding, God, without any merit of mine, but only of mere grace, grants and imputes to me, the perfect satisfaction, righteousness and holiness of Christ;

189

even so, as if I never had had, nor committed any sin: yea, as if I had fully accomplished all that obedience which Christ has accomplished for me; inasmuch as I embrace such benefit with a believing heart.

(Scripture proofs: Rom. 3:22ff; Gal. 2:16; Eph. 2:8, 9; Rom. 3:9ff; Rom. 7:23; Rom. 3:24; Tit. 3:5; Eph. 2:8, 9; Rom. 4:4, 5; 2 Cor. 5:19; 1 John 2:1; Rom. 3:24, 25; 2 Cor. 5:21; Rom. 3:28; John 3:18.)

f. Lord's Day 51
Question and Answer 126
Q. Which is the fifth petition [of the Lord's Prayer]?
A. "And forgive us our debts as we forgive our debtors"; that is, be pleased for the sake of Christ's blood, not to impute to us poor sinners, our transgressions, nor *that depravity, which always cleaves to us;* even as we feel this evidence of thy grace in us, that it is our firm resolution from the heart to forgive our neighbor.

(Scripture proofs: Matt. 6:12; Ps. 51:1; 1 John 2:1, 2; Matt. 6:14, 15.)

2. (BELGIC) CONFESSION OF FAITH
a. Article 14

We believe that God created man out of the dust of the earth, and made and formed him after his own image and likeness, good, righteous, and holy, capable in all things to will, agreeably to the will of God. But being in honor, he understood it not, neither knew his excellency, but willfully subjected himself to sin, and consequently to death, and the curse, giving ear to the words of the devil. For the commandment of life, which he had received, he transgressed; and by sin separated himself from God, who was his true life, *having corrupted his whole nature;* whereby he *made himself liable to corporal and spiritual death.* And being thus *become wicked, perverse, and corrupt in all his ways,* he hath *lost all his excellent gifts,* which he had received from God, and only retained a few remains thereof, which, however, are sufficient to leave man without excuse; for all the light which is in us is changed into darkness, as the Scriptures teach us, saying: The light shineth in darkness, and the darkness comprehendeth it not: where St. John calleth men darkness. Therefore we reject all that is taught repugnant to this, concerning the free will of man, since man is but a slave to sin; and hath nothing of himself, unless it is given from heaven. For who may presume to boast, that he of himself can do any good, since Christ saith, *No man* can come to me, except the Father, which hath sent me, draw him? Who will glory in his own will, who understands, that to be carnally minded is *enmity* against God? Who can speak of his knowledge, since the natural man receiveth not the things of the spirit of God? In short, who dare suggest any thought, since he knows that we are not sufficient of ourselves to think anything as of ourselves, but that our sufficiency is of God? And therefore what the apostle saith ought justly to be held sure and firm, that God worketh in us both to will and to do of his good pleasure. For there is *no will or understanding, conformable to the divine will and understanding,* but what Christ hath wrought in man; which he teaches us, when he saith, Without me ye can do *nothing.*

b. Article 15

We believe that, through the disobedience of Adam, original sin is extended to *all mankind;* which is a corruption of the *whole nature,* and an hereditary disease, wherewith infants themselves are infected even in their mother's womb, and which produceth in man all sorts of sin, being in him as a root thereof; and therefore is so vile and abominable in the sight of God, that it is sufficient to condemn *all mankind.* Nor is it by any means abolished or done away by baptism; since sin always issues forth from this woeful source, as water from a fountain; notwithstanding it is not imputed to the children of God unto condemnation, but by his grace and mercy is forgiven them. Not that they should rest securely in sin, but that a sense of this corruption should make believers often to sigh, desiring to be delivered from this body of death. Wherefore we reject the error of the Pelagians, who assert that sin proceeds only from imitation.

The following two articles of the Belgic Confession of Faith demonstrate the relationship between the doctrine of total depravity and the other four points, that is, since men are totally depraved, salvation must be, and is, all of grace in all its parts.

c. Article 16

We believe that *all the posterity of Adam* being thus *fallen into perdition and ruin,* by the sin of our first parents, God then did manifest himself such as he is; that is to say, merciful and just: Merciful, since he delivers and preserves from this perdition all, whom he, in his eternal and unchangeable counsel of mere goodness, hath elected in Christ Jesus our Lord, without any respect to their works: Just, in leaving others in the fall and perdition wherein they have involved themselves.

d. Article 17

We believe that our most gracious God, in his admirable wisdom and goodness, seeing that man had thus thrown himself into *temporal and eternal death,* and made himself *wholly miserable,* was pleased to seek and comfort him, when he trembling fled from his presence, promising him that he would give his Son, who should be made of a woman, to bruise the head of the serpent, and would make him happy.

3. CANONS OF DORDT
  a. First Head of Doctrine, Article 1

As all men have sinned in Adam, *lie under the curse,* and are *deserving of eternal death,* God would have done no injustice by leaving them all to perish, and delivering them over to condemnation on account of sin, according to the words of the apostle, Rom. 3:19, "that every mouth may be stopped, and *all* the world may become guilty before God." And verse 23: "for *all* have sinned, and come short of the glory of God." And Rom. 6:23: "for the wages of sin is death."

It should be noted that each section of the Canons is divided into two parts, a positive section in which each doctrine is explained and a negative section in which various errors are condemned and rejected. These sections are valuable not only because they help in sharply and clearly defining the truths under discussion, but also because they contain many proof texts for these truths.

b. First Head of Doctrine, Rejection of Errors, Error 4

The true doctrine concerning Election and Rejection having been explained, the Synod rejects the errors of those who teach: That in the election unto faith this condition is beforehand demanded, viz., that man should use the light of nature aright, be pious, humble, meek, and fit for eternal life, as if on these things election were in any way dependent. For this savors of the teaching of Pelagius, and is opposed to the doctrine of the apostle, when he writes: *"Among whom we also all once lived in the lust of our flesh, doing the desires of the flesh and of the mind, and were by nature children of wrath, even as the rest;* but God being rich in mercy, for his great love wherewith he loved us, even when we were dead through our trespasses, made us alive together with Christ (by grace have ye been saved), and raised us up with him, and made us to sit with him in heavenly places, in Christ Jesus; that in the ages to come he might show the exceeding riches of his grace in kindness towards us in Christ Jesus; for by grace have ye been saved through faith; and that not of yourselves, it is the gift of God; not of works, that no man should glory" (Eph. 2:3–9).

c. Third and Fourth Heads of Doctrine, Article 1

Man was originally formed after the image of God. His understanding was adorned with a true and saving knowledge of his Creator, and of spiritual things; his heart and will were upright; all his affections pure; and the whole man was holy; but revolting from God by the instigation of the devil, and abusing the freedom of his own will, he forfeited these excellent gifts; and on the contrary entailed on himself *blindness of mind, horrible darkness, vanity and perverseness of judgment,* became *wicked, rebellious, and obdurate in heart and will, and impure in his affections.*

d. Third and Fourth Heads of Doctrine, Article 2

Man after the fall begat children in his own likeness. A *corrupt stock* produced a *corrupt offspring.* Hence *all the posterity of Adam,* Christ only excepted, have derived corruption from their original parent, not by imitation, as the

Pelagians of old asserted, but by the propagation of a *vicious nature.*

e. Third and Fourth Heads of Doctrine, Article 3

Therefore all men are conceived in sin, and by nature children of wrath, incapable of saving good, prone to evil, dead in sin, and in bondage thereto, and without the regenerating grace of the Holy Spirit, *they are neither able nor willing to return to God, to reform the depravity of their nature, nor to dispose themselves to reformation.*

f. Third and Fourth Heads of Doctrine, Article 4

There remain, however, in man since the fall, the glimmerings of natural light, whereby he retains some knowledge of God, of natural things, and of the difference between good and evil, and discovers some regard for virtue, good order in society, and for maintaining an orderly external deportment. But so far is this light of nature from being sufficient to bring him to a saving knowledge of God, and to true conversion, that he is *incapable of using it aright even in things natural and civil.* Nay further, this light, such as it is, man in various ways renders *wholly polluted,* and holds it in unrighteousness, by doing which he becomes inexcusable before God.

g. Third and Fourth Heads of Doctrine, Rejection of Errors, Error 1

The true doctrine having been explained, the Synod rejects the errors of those who teach: That it cannot properly be said, that original sin in itself suffices to condemn the whole human race, or to deserve temporal and eternal punishment. For these contradict the Apostle, who declares: "Therefore as through one man sin entered into the world, and death through sin, and so *death passed unto all men, for that all sinned*" (Rom. 5:12). And: "The judgment came of one unto condemnation" (Rom. 5:16). And: "The wages of sin is death" (Rom. 6:23).

h. Third and Fourth Heads of Doctrine, Rejection of Errors, Error 2

The true doctrine having been explained, the Synod rejects the errors of those who teach: That the spiritual gifts, or the good qualities and virtues, such as: goodness, holiness, righteousness, could not belong to the will of man when he was first created, and that these, therefore, could not have been separated therefrom in the fall. For such is contrary to the description of the image of God, which the Apostle gives in Eph. 4:24, where he declares that it consists in righteousness and holiness, which undoubtedly belong to the will.

i. Third and Fourth Heads of Doctrine, Rejection of Errors, Error 3.

The true doctrine having been explained, the Synod rejects the errors of those who teach: That in spiritual death the spiritual gifts are not separate from the will of man, since the will in itself has never been corrupted, but only hindered through the darkness of the understanding and the irregularity of the affections; and that, these hindrances having been removed, the will can then bring into operation its native powers, that is, that the will of itself is able to will and to choose, or not to will and not to choose, all manner of good which may be presented to it. This is an innovation and an error, and tends to elevate the powers of the free will, contrary to the declaration of the Prophet: *"The heart is deceitful above all things, and it is exceedingly corrupt"* (Jer. 17:9); and of the Apostle: "Among whom (sons of disobedience) we also all once lived in the lusts of the flesh, doing the desires of the flesh and of the mind" (Eph. 2:3).

j. Third and Fourth Heads of Doctrine, Rejection of Errors, Error 4

The true doctrine having been explained, the Synod rejects the errors of those who teach: That the unregenerate man is not really nor utterly dead in sin, nor destitute of all powers unto spiritual good, but that he can yet hunger and thirst after righteousness and life, and offer the sacrifice of a contrite and broken spirit, which is pleasing to God. For these are

195

contrary to the express testimony of Scripture. *"Ye were dead through trespasses and sins"* (Eph. 2:1, 5); and: *"Every imagination of the thoughts of his heart are only evil continually"* (Gen. 6:5; Gen. 8:21).

Moreover, to hunger and thirst after deliverance from misery, and after life, and to offer unto God the sacrifice of a broken spirit, is peculiar to the regenerate and those that are called blessed (Ps. 51:10, 19; Matt. 5:6).

k. Third and Fourth Heads of Doctrine, Rejection of Errors, Error 5

The true doctrine having been explained, the Synod rejects the errors of those who teach: That the corrupt and natural man can so well use the common grace (by which they understand the light of nature), or the gifts still left him after the fall, that he can gradually gain by their good use a greater, viz., the evangelical or saving grace and salvation itself. And that in this way God on his part shows himself ready to reveal Christ unto all men, since he applies to all sufficiently and efficiently the means necessary to conversion. For the experience of all ages and the Scriptures do both testify that this is untrue. "He showeth his Word unto Jacob, his statutes and his ordinances unto Israel. He hath not dealt so with any nation: and as for his ordinances they have not known them" (Ps. 147:19, 20). "Who in the generations gone by suffered all the nations to walk in their own way" (Acts 14:16). And: "And they (Paul and his companions) having been forbidden of the Holy Spirit to speak the word in Asia, and when they were come over against Mysia, they assayed to go into Bithynia, and the Spirit suffered them not" (Acts 16:6, 7).

4. WESTMINSTER CONFESSION OF FAITH
a. Chapter 6, Article 1

Our first parents being *seduced* by the subtilty and temptation of Satan, sinned in eating the forbidden fruit. This their sin God was pleased, according to his wise and holy counsel, to permit, having purposed to order it to His own glory.

(Scripture proofs: Gen. 3:13; 2 Cor. 11:3; Rom. 11:32.)

b. Chapter 6, Article 2

By this sin they fell from their original righteousness, and communion with God, and so became *dead in sin, and wholly defiled in all the faculties and parts of soul and body.*

(Scripture proofs: Gen. 3:6–8; Eccl. 7:29; Rom. 3:23; Gen. 2:17; Eph. 2:1; Tit. 1:15; Gen. 6:5; Jer. 17:9; Rom. 3:10–18.)

c. Chapter 6, Article 3

They being the root of all mankind, the guilt of this sin was imputed, and the same *death in sin* and *corrupted nature* conveyed to *all their posterity,* descending from them by ordinary generation.

(Scripture proofs: Gen. 1:27, 28; Gen. 2:16, 17; Acts 17:26 with Rom. 5:12, 15–19; 1 Cor. 15:21, 22, 45, 49; Ps. 51:5; Gen. 5:3; Job 14:4; Job 15:14.)

d. Chapter 6, Article 4

From this original corruption, whereby *we are utterly indisposed, disabled, and made opposite to all good, and wholly inclined to all evil,* do proceed all actual transgressions.

(Scripture proofs: Rom. 5:6; Rom. 8:7; Rom. 7:18; Col. 1:21; Gen. 6:5; Gen. 8:21; Rom. 3:10–12; James 1:14, 15; Eph. 2:2, 3; Matt. 15:19.)

e. Chapter 6, Article 5

This *corruption of nature,* during this life, doth remain in those that are regenerated: and although it be through Christ pardoned and mortified, yet both itself, and all the motions thereof, are truly and properly sin.

(Scripture proofs: 1 John 1:8, 10; Rom. 7:14, 17, 18, 23; James 3:2; Prov. 20:9; Eccl. 7:20; Rom. 7:5, 7, 8, 25; Gal. 5:17.)

f. Chapter 6, Article 6

Every sin, both original and actual, being a transgression of the righteous law of God, and contrary thereunto, doth, in its own nature, bring guilt upon the sinner, whereby he is *bound over to the wrath of God, and curse of the law, and so made subject to death, with all miseries spiritual, temporal, and eternal.*

(Scripture proofs: 1 John 3:4; Rom. 2:15; Rom. 3:9, 19; Eph. 2:3; Gal. 3:10; Rom. 6:23; Eph. 4:18; Rom. 8:20; Matt. 25:41; 2 Thess. 1:9.)

g. Chapter 9, Article 3

Man, by his fall into a state of sin, hath *wholly lost all ability of will to any spiritual good* accompanying salvation; so as a natural man, *being altogether averse from that good, and dead in sin,* is *not able,* by his own strength, to convert himself, or to prepare himself thereunto.

(Scripture proofs: Rom. 5:6; Rom. 8:7; John 15:5; Rom. 3:10, 12; Eph. 2:1, 5; Col. 2:13; John 6:44, 65; Eph. 2:2–5; 1 Cor. 2:14; Tit. 3:3–5.)

h. Chapter 9, Article 4

When God converts a sinner, and translates him into the state of grace, he freeth him from his *natural bondage* under sin; and by his grace alone enables him freely to will and to do that which is spiritually good; yet so as that, by reason of his remaining corruption, he doth not perfectly nor only will that which is good, but doth also will that which is evil.

(Scripture proofs: Col. 1:13; John 8:34, 36; Phil. 2:13; Rom. 6:18, 22; Gal. 5:17; Rom. 7:15, 18, 19, 21, 23.)

i. Chapter 9, Article 5

The will of man is made perfectly and immutably *free to do good alone in the state of glory only.*

(Scripture proofs: Eph. 4:13; Heb. 12:23; 1 John 3:2; Jude 24.)

j. Chapter 16, Article 7

Works done by unregenerate men, although, for the matter of them, they may be things which God commands, and of good use both to themselves and others; yet, because they proceed not from an heart purified by faith; nor are done in a right manner, according to the word; nor to a right end, the glory of God; they are therefore sinful, and *cannot please God,* or make a man meet to receive grace from God. And yet their neglect of them is more sinful, and displeasing unto God.

(Scripture proofs: 2 Kings 10:30, 31; 1 Kings 21:27, 29; Phil. 1:15, 16, 18; Gen. 4:5; Heb. 11:4, 6; 1 Cor. 13:3; Isa. 1:12; Matt. 6:2, 5, 16; Hag. 2:14; Tit. 1:15; Amos 5:21, 22; Hos. 1:4; Rom. 9:16; Tit. 3:15; Ps. 14:4; Ps. 36:3; Job 21:14, 15; Matt. 25:41–43, 45; Matt. 23:3.)

5. WESTMINSTER LARGER CATECHISM

a. *Question and Answer 25*

Q. Wherein consisteth the sinfulness of that estate whereinto man fell?

A. The sinfulness of that estate whereinto man fell, consisteth in the *guilt of Adam's first sin,* the *want of that righteousness wherein he was created,* and the *corruption of his nature,* whereby he is *utterly indisposed, disabled, and made opposite unto all that is spiritually good,* and *wholly inclined to all evil,* and that continually; which is commonly called Original Sin, and from which do proceed all actual transgressions.

(Scripture proofs: Rom. 5:12, 19; Rom. 3:10–19; Eph. 2:1–3; Rom. 5:6; Rom. 8:7, 8; Gen. 6:5; James 1:14, 15; Matt. 15:19.)

b. *Question and Answer 27*

Q. What misery did the fall bring upon mankind?

A. The fall brought upon mankind the loss of communion with God, his displeasure and curse; so as *we are by nature children of wrath, bond slaves to Satan,* and justly liable to the punishments in this world, and that which is to come.

(Scripture proofs: Gen. 3:8, 10, 24; Eph. 2:2, 3; 2 Tim. 2:26; Gen. 2:17; Lam. 3:39; Rom. 6:23; Matt. 15:41, 46; Jude 7.)

c. *Question and Answer 149*

Q. Is any man able perfectly to keep the commandments of God?

A. *No man is able,* either of himself, or by any grace received in this life, perfectly to keep the commandments of God; but doth *daily* break them in thought, word, and deed.

(Scripture proofs: Jam. 3:2; John 15:5; Rom. 8:3; Eccl. 7:20; 1 John 1:8, 10; Gal. 5:17; Rom. 7:18, 19; Gen. 6:5; Gen. 8:21; Rom. 3:9–19; James 3:2–13.)

C. UNCONDITIONAL ELECTION

1. HEIDELBERG CATECHISM

a. Lord's Day 21

Question and Answer 54

Q. What believest thou concerning the "holy catholic church" of Christ?

A. That the Son of God from the beginning to the end of the world, gathers, defends, and preserves to himself by his Spir-

it and word, out of the whole human race, a church *chosen
to everlasting life,* agreeing in true faith; and that I am and
for ever shall remain, a living member thereof.

(Scripture proofs: John 10:11; Gen. 26:4; Rom. 9:24; Eph. 1:10; John 10:16;
Isa. 59:21; Deut. 10:14, 15; Acts 13:48; 1 Cor. 1:8, 9; Rom. 8:35ff.)

2. (BELGIC) CONFESSION OF FAITH
a. Article 16

We believe that all the posterity of Adam being thus fallen
into perdition and ruin, by the sin of our first parents, God
then did manifest himself such as he is; that is to say, merciful
and just: Merciful, since he delivers and preserves from this
perdition *all, whom he, in his eternal and unchangeable counsel of mere goodness, hath elected in Christ Jesus our Lord,
without any respect to their works:* Just, in leaving others in
the fall and perdition wherein they have involved themselves.

3. CANONS OF DORDT
a. First Head of Doctrine, Article 6

That some receive the gift of faith from God, and others
do not receive it proceeds from *God's eternal decree,* "For
known unto God are all his works from the beginning of the
world" (Acts 15:18). "Who worketh all things after the counsel of his will" (Eph. 1:11). According to which *decree,* he
graciously softens the hearts of the elect, however obstinate,
and inclines them to believe, while he leaves the non-elect in
his just judgment to their own wickedness and obduracy. And
herein is especially displayed the profound, the merciful, and
at the same time the righteous discrimination between men,
equally involved in ruin; or that decree of election and reprobation, revealed in the Word of God, which though men of
perverse, impure, and unstable minds wrest to their own destruction, yet to holy and pious souls affords unspeakable
consolation.

b. First Head of Doctrine, Article 7

Election is the unchangeable purpose of God, whereby, before the foundation of the world, he hath out of mere grace,
according to the sovereign good pleasure of his own will, chosen, from the whole human race, which had fallen through

their own fault, from their primitive state of rectitude, into sin and destruction, a certain number of persons to redemption in Christ, whom he from eternity appointed the Mediator and Head of the elect, and the foundation of salvation.

This elect number, though by nature neither better nor more deserving than others, but with them involved in one common misery, *God hath decreed to give to Christ, to be saved by him,* and effectually to call and draw them to his communion by his Word and Spirit, to bestow upon them true faith, justification and sanctification; and having powerfully preserved them in the fellowship of his Son, finally, to glorify them for the demonstration of his mercy, and for the praise of his glorious grace; as it is written: "According as he hath chosen us in him, before the foundation of the world, that we should be holy, and without blame before him in love; having predestinated us unto the adoption of children by Jesus Christ to himself, according to the good pleasure of his will, to the praise of the glory of his grace, wherein he hath made us accepted in the beloved" (Eph. 1:4–6). And elsewhere: "Whom he did predestinate, them he also called, and whom he called, them he also justified, and whom he justified, them he also glorified" (Rom. 8:30).

c. First Head of Doctrine, Article 9

This election was not founded upon foreseen faith, and the obedience of faith, holiness, or any other good quality or disposition in man, as the pre-requisite, cause or condition on which it depended; but men are chosen to faith and to the obedience of faith, holiness, etc., therefore election is the fountain of every saving good; from which proceed faith, holiness, and the other gifts of salvation, and finally eternal life itself, as its fruits and effects, according to that of the apostle: "He hath chosen us (not because we were) but that we should be holy, and without blame, before him in love" (Eph. 1:4).

d. First Head of Doctrine, Article 10

The good pleasure of God is the sole cause of this gracious election; which doth not consist herein, that out of all possi-

ble qualities and actions of men God has chosen some as a
condition of salvation; but that he was pleased out of the
common mass of sinners to adopt some certain persons as a
peculiar people to himself, as it is written, "For the children
being not yet born neither having done any good or evil,"
etc., it was said (namely to Rebecca): "the elder shall serve
the younger; as it is written, Jacob have I loved, but Esau have
I hated" (Rom. 9:11–13). "And as many as were ordained to
eternal life believed" (Acts 13:48).

e. First Head of Doctrine, Article 11
    And as God himself is most wise, unchangeable, omni-
scient and omnipotent, so the election made by him can neither be interrupted nor changed, recalled or annulled; neither
can the elect be cast away, nor their number diminished.

f. First Head of Doctrine, Article 15
    What peculiarly tends to illustrate and recommend to us
the eternal and unmerited grace of election, is the express testimony of sacred Scripture, that not all, but *some only are
elected,* while others are passed by in the eternal decree;
whom God, out of his sovereign, most just, irreprehensible
and unchangeable good pleasure, hath decreed to leave in the
common misery into which they have wilfully plunged themselves, and not to bestow upon them saving faith and the
grace of conversion; but permitting them in his just judgment
to follow their own ways, at last for the declaration of his justice, to condemn and perish them forever, not only on account of their unbelief, but also for all their other sins. And
this is the *decree of reprobation* which by no means makes
God the author of sin (the very thought of which is blasphemy), but declares him to be an awful, irreprehensible, and
righteous judge and avenger thereof.

g. First Head of Doctrine, Rejection of Errors, Error 1
    The true doctrine concerning Election and Rejection hav-
ing been explained, the Synod rejects the errors of those who
teach: That the will of God to save those who would believe
and would persevere in faith and in the obedience of faith, is

the whole and entire decree of election unto salvation, and that nothing else concerning this decree has been revealed in God's Word.

For these deceive the simple and plainly contradict the Scriptures, which declare that God will not only save those who will believe, but that he has also from eternity chosen certain particular persons to whom above others he in time will grant both faith in Christ and perseverance; as it is written: "I manifested thy name unto the men whom thou gavest me out of the world" (John 17:6). "And as many as were ordained to eternal life believed" (Acts 13:48). And: "Even as he chose us in him before the foundation of the world, that we should be holy and without blemish before him in love" (Eph. 1:4).

h. First Head of Doctrine, Rejection of Errors, Error 2

The true doctrine concerning Election and Rejection having been explained, the Synod rejects the errors of those who teach: That there are various kinds of election of God unto eternal life: the one general and indefinite, the other particular and definite; and that the latter in turn is either incomplete, revocable, non-decisive and conditional, or complete, irrevocable, decisive and absolute. Likewise: that there is one election unto faith, and another unto salvation, so that election can be unto justifying faith, without being a decisive election unto salvation. For this is a fancy of men's minds, invented regardless of the Scriptures, whereby the doctrine of election is corrupted, and this golden chain of our salvation is broken: "And whom he foreordained, them he also called; and whom he called, them he also justified; and whom he justified, them he also glorified" (Rom. 8:30).

i. First Head of Doctrine, Rejection of Errors, Error 3

The true doctrine concerning Election and Rejection having been explained, the Synod rejects the errors of those who teach: That the good pleasure and purpose of God, of which Scripture makes mention in the doctrine of election, does not consist in this, that God chose certain persons rather than others, but in this, that he chose out of all possible conditions (among which are also the works of the law), or out of the whole order of things, the act of faith which from its very nature is undeserving, as well as its incomplete obedience, as a condition of salvation, and that he would graciously consider this in itself as a complete obedience and count it worthy of the reward of eternal life. For by this injurious error the pleasure of God and the merits of Christ are made of none effect, and men are drawn away by useless questions from the truth of gracious justification and from the simplicity of Scripture, and this declaration of the Apostle is charged as untrue: "Who saved us, and called us with a holy calling, not according to our works, but according to his own purpose and grace, which was given us in Christ Jesus before times eternal" (2 Tim. 1:9).

j. First Head of Doctrine, Rejection of Errors, Error 4

The true doctrine concerning Election and Rejection having been explained, the Synod rejects the errors of those who teach: That in the election unto faith this condition is beforehand demanded, viz., that man should use the light of nature aright, be pious, humble, meek, and fit for eternal life, as if on these things election were in any way dependent. For this savors of the teaching of Pelagius, and is opposed to the doctrine of the apostle, when he writes: "Among whom we also all once lived in the lust of our flesh, doing the desires of the flesh and of the mind, and were by nature children of wrath, even as the rest; but God being rich in mercy, for his great love wherewith he loved us, even when we were dead through our trespasses, made us alive together with Christ (by grace have ye been saved), and raised us up with him, and made us to sit with him in heavenly places, in Christ Jesus; that in the ages to come he might show the exceeding riches of his grace in kindness towards us in Christ Jesus; for by grace have ye been saved through faith; and that not of yourselves, it is the gift of God; not of works, that no man should glory" (Eph. 2:3–9).

k. First Head of Doctrine, Rejection of Errors, Error 5

The true doctrine concerning Election and Rejection having been explained, the Synod rejects the errors of those who teach: That the incomplete and non-decisive election of particular persons to salvation occurred because of a foreseen faith, conversion, holiness, godliness, which either began or continued for some time; but that the complete and decisive election occurred because of foreseen perseverance unto the end in faith, conversion, holiness and godliness; and that this is the gracious and evangelical worthiness, for the sake of which he who is chosen, is more worthy than he who is not chosen; and that therefore faith, the obedience of faith, holiness, godliness and perseverance are not fruits of the unchangeable election unto glory, but are conditions, which, being required beforehand, were foreseen as being met by those who will be fully elected, and are causes without which the unchangeable election to glory does not occur.

This is repugnant to the entire Scripture, which constantly inculcates this and similar declarations: Election is not of works, but of him that calleth (Rom. 9:11). "And as many as were ordained to eternal life believed" (Acts 13:48). "He chose us in him before the foundation of the world, that we should be holy" (Eph. 1:4). "Ye did not choose me, but I chose you" (John 15:16). "But if it be of grace, it is no more of works" (Rom. 11:6). "Herein is love, not that we loved God, but that he loved us, and sent his Son" (1 John 4:10).

I. First Head of Doctrine, Rejection of Errors, Error 6
    The true doctrine concerning Election and Rejection having been explained, the Synod rejects the errors of those who teach: That not every election unto salvation is unchangeable, but that some of the elect, any decree of God notwithstanding, can yet perish and do indeed perish. By which gross error they make God to be changeable, and destroy the comfort which the godly obtain out of the firmness of their election, and contradict the Holy Scripture, which teaches, that the elect can not be led astray (Matt. 24:24); that Christ does not lose those whom the Father gave him (John 6:39); and that God hath also glorified those whom he foreordained, called and justified (Rom. 8:30).

The next four articles from the Canons of Dordt show the relationship between unconditional election and limited atonement, that is, that Christ died for the elect.

m. Second Head of Doctrine, Article 8

For this was *the sovereign counsel, and most gracious will and purpose of God the Father,* that the quickening and saving efficacy of the most precious death of his Son should extend to all the elect, for bestowing on them alone the gift of justifying faith, thereby to bring them infallibly to salvation: that is, it was the will of God, that Christ by the blood of the cross, whereby he confirmed the new covenant, should effectually redeem out of every people, tribe, nation, and language, all those, and those only, *who were from eternity chosen to salvation,* and given to him by the Father; that he should confer upon them faith, which together with all the other saving gifts of the Holy Spirit, he purchased for them by his death; should purge them from all sin, both original and actual, whether committed before or after believing; and having faithfully preserved them even to the end, should at last bring them free from every spot and blemish to the enjoyment of glory in his own presence forever.

n. Second Head of Doctrine, Article 9

This *purpose* proceeding from *everlasting love towards the elect,* has from the beginning of the world to this day been powerfully accomplished, and will henceforward still continue to be accomplished, notwithstanding all the ineffectual opposition of the gates of hell, so that the elect in due time may be gathered together into one, and that there never may be wanting a church composed of believers, the foundation of which is laid in the blood of Christ, which may steadfastly love, and faithfully serve him as their Savior, who as a bridegroom for his bride, laid down his life for them upon the cross, and which may celebrate his praises here and through all eternity.

o. Second Head of Doctrine, Rejection of Errors, Error 1

The true doctrine having been explained, the Synod rejects the errors of those who teach: That God the Father has ordained his Son to the death of the cross without a certain and definite decree to save any, so that the necessity, profitableness and worth of what Christ merited by his death might have existed, and might remain in all its parts complete, perfect and intact, even if the merited redemption had never in fact been applied to any person. For this doctrine tends to the despising of the wisdom of the Father and of the merits of Jesus Christ, and is contrary to Scripture. For thus saith our Savior: "I lay down my life for the sheep, and I know them" (John 10:15, 27). And the prophet Isaiah saith concerning the Savior: "When thou shalt make his soul an offering for sin, he shall see his seed, he shall prolong his days, and the pleasure of Jehovah shall prosper in his hand" (Isa. 53:10). Finally, this contradicts the article of faith according to which we believe the catholic Christian church.

p. Second Head of Doctrine, Rejection of Errors, Error 7

The true doctrine having been explained, the Synod rejects the errors of those who teach: That Christ neither could die, needed to die, nor did die for those whom God loved in the highest degree and elected to eternal life, and did not die for these, since these do not need the death of Christ. For they contradict the Apostle, who declares: "Christ loved me, and gave himself for me" (Gal. 2:20). Likewise: "Who shall lay any thing to the charge of God's elect? It is God that justifieth; who is he that condemneth? It is Christ Jesus that died" (Rom. 8:33, 34), viz., for them; and the Savior who says: "I lay down my life for the sheep" (John 10:15). And: "This is my commandment, that ye love one another, even as I have loved you. Greater love hath no man than this, that a man lay down his life for his friends" (John 15:12, 13).

The last four articles from the Canons, quoted below, show how unconditional election is fulfilled and carried out by irresistible grace and the preservation of saints.

q. Third and Fourth Heads of Doctrine, Article 10

But that others who are called by the gospel, obey the call, and are converted, is not to be ascribed to the proper exercise of free will, whereby one distinguishes himself above others, equally furnished with grace sufficient for faith and conversions, as the proud heresy of Pelagius maintains; but it must be wholly ascribed to God, who as *he has chosen his own from eternity in Christ,* so he confers upon them faith and repentance, rescues them from the power of darkness, and translates them into the kingdom of his own Son, that they may show forth the praises of him, who hath called them out of darkness into his marvelous light; and may glory not in themselves, but in the Lord according to the testimony of the apostles in various places.

r.   Fifth Head of Doctrine, Article 6
     But God, who is rich in mercy, according to his *unchangeable purpose of election,* does not wholly withdraw the Holy Spirit from his own people, even in their melancholy falls; nor suffers them to proceed so far as to lose the grace of adoption, and forfeit the state of justification, or to commit the sin unto death; nor does he permit them to be totally deserted, and to plunge themselves into everlasting destruction.

s.   Fifth Head of Doctrine, Article 8
     Thus, it is not in consequence of their own merits, or strength, but of God's free mercy, that they do not totally fall from faith and grace, nor continue and perish finally in their backslidings; which, with respect to themselves, is not only possible, but would undoubtedly happen; but with respect to God, it is utterly impossible, since *his counsel cannot be changed,* nor his promise fail, neither can the call according to his purpose be revoked, nor the merit, intercession and preservation of Christ be rendered ineffectual, nor the sealing of the Holy Spirit be frustrated or obliterated.

t.   Fifth Head of Doctrine, Rejection of Errors, Error 1
     The true doctrine having been explained, the Synod rejects the errors of those who teach: That the perseverance of the true believers is not a fruit of election, or a gift of God, gained by the death of Christ, but a condition of the new

covenant, which (as they declare) man before his decisive election and justification must fulfill through his free will. For the Holy Scripture testifies that this follows out of election, and is given the elect in virtue of the death, the resurrection and intercession of Christ: "But the elect obtained it and the rest were hardened" (Rom. 11:7). Likewise: "He that spared not his own Son, but delivered him up for us all, how shall he not also with him freely give us all things? Who shall lay anything to the charge of God's elect? It is God that justifieth; who is he that condemneth? It is Christ Jesus that died, yea rather, that was raised from the dead, who is at the right hand of God, who also maketh intercession for us. Who shall separate us from the love of Christ?" (Rom. 8:32–35).

4. WESTMINSTER CONFESSION OF FAITH
a. Chapter 3, Article 6

As God hath *appointed the elect* unto glory, so hath he, by *the eternal and most free purpose of his will,* foreordained all the means thereunto. Wherefore they who are elected being fallen in Adam, are redeemed by Christ; are effectually called unto faith in Christ by his Spirit working in due season; are justified, adopted, sanctified, and kept by his power through faith unto salvation. Neither are any others redeemed by Christ, effectually called, justified, adopted, sanctified, and saved, but *the elect only.*

(Scripture proofs: 1 Pet. 1:2; Eph. 1:4, 5; Eph. 2:10; 2 Thess. 2:13; 1 Thess. 5:9, 10; Tit. 2:14; Rom. 8:30; Eph. 1:5; 2 Thess. 2:13; 1 Pet. 1:5; John 17:9; Rom. 8:28; John 6:64, 65; John 10:26; John 8:47; 1 John 2:19.)

b. Chapter 11, Article 4

God did, from all eternity, decree to justify all the elect; and Christ did, in the fulness of time, die for their sins, and rise again for their justification: nevertheless they are not justified, until the Holy Spirit doth in due time actually apply Christ unto them.

(Scripture proofs: Gal. 3:8; 1 Pet. 1:2, 19, 20; Rom. 8:30; Gal. 4:4; 1 Tim. 2:6; Rom. 4:25; Col. 1:21, 22; Gal. 2:16; Tit. 3:4–7.)

5. WESTMINSTER LARGER CATECHISM

a. *Question and Answer 12*
Q. What are the decrees of God?
A. God's decrees are the wise, free, and holy acts of the counsel of his will, whereby, from all eternity, *he hath, for his own glory, unchangeably foreordained whatsoever comes to pass in time,* especially concerning angels and men.
(Scripture proofs: Eph. 1:11; Rom. 11:33; Rom. 9:14, 15, 18; Eph. 1:4, 11; Rom. 9:22, 23; Ps. 33:11.)

b. *Question and Answer 13*
Q. What hath God especially decreed concerning angels and men?
A. *God, by an eternal and immutable decree,* out of his mere love, for the praise of his glorious grace, to be manifested in due time, hath elected some angels to glory; and in Christ hath chosen some men to eternal life, and the means thereof: and also, according to his sovereign power, and the unsearchable counsel of his own will (whereby He extendeth or withholdeth favour as He pleaseth), hath passed by and foreordained the rest to dishonour and wrath, to be for their sin inflicted, to the praise of the glory of his justice.
(Scripture proofs: 1 Tim. 5:21; Eph. 1:4–6; 2 Thess. 2:13, 14; Rom. 9:17, 18, 21, 22; Matt. 11:25, 26; 2 Tim. 2:20; Jude 4; 1 Pet. 2:8.)

c. *Question and Answer 14*
Q. How doth God execute his decrees?
A. God executeth his decrees in the works of creation and providence, according to his infallible foreknowledge, and *the free and immutable counsel of his own will.*
(Scripture proof: Eph. 1:11.)

D. LIMITED ATONEMENT

1. HEIDELBERG CATECHISM

a. Lord's Day 11
Question and Answer 29
Q. Why is the Son of God called Jesus, that is a Savior?
A. Because he saveth *us,* and delivereth *us* from our sins; and likewise, because we ought not to seek, neither can find salvation in any other.
(Scripture proofs: Matt. 1:21; Acts 4:12.)

In the preceding quotation we have an excellent example of many articles in all the creeds that use the words "we" and "us" to describe those who benefit from Christ's death—words that are by their very nature exclusive and not inclusive.

Though the next article does not directly answer the question "For whom did Christ die?" it nonetheless supports the doctrine of limited atonement by insisting that those for whom Christ died are *completely* saved in Him and that salvation is not just made possible for them. In fact, the Belgic Confession Article 22 quotation (#2 below) calls a gross blasphemy the idea that Christ makes salvation only "possible."

    b. Lord's Day 11

    Question and Answer 30

    Q. Do such then believe in Jesus the only Savior, who seek their salvation and welfare of saints, or themselves, or anywhere else?

    A. They do not; for though they boast of him in words, yet in deeds they deny Jesus the only deliverer and Savior; for one of these two things must be true, that either Jesus is not a *complete Savior;* or that they, who by a true faith receive this Savior, must find all things in him necessary to their *salvation.*

    (Scripture proofs: 1 Cor. 1:13, 31; Gal. 5:4; Col. 2:20; Isa. 9:6, 7; Col. 1:19, 20.)

    c. Lord's Day 21

    Question and Answer 54

    Q. What believest thou concerning the "holy catholic church" of Christ?

    A. That the Son of God from the beginning to the end of the world, gathers, defends, and preserves to himself by his Spirit and word, out of the whole human race, *a church chosen to everlasting life,* agreeing in true faith; and that I am and for ever shall remain, a living member thereof.

    (Scripture proofs: John 10:11; Gen. 26:4; Rom. 9:24; Eph. 1:10, John 10:16; Isa. 59:21; Deut. 10:14, 15; Acts 13:48; 1 Cor. 1:8, 9; Rom. 8:35ff.)

2. (BELGIC) CONFESSION OF FAITH

    a. Article 22

    We believe that, to attain the true knowledge of this great mystery, the Holy Ghost kindleth in our hearts an upright faith, which embraces Jesus Christ, with all his merits, appropriates him, and seeks nothing more besides him. For it must needs follow, either that all things, which are requisite to our salvation, are not in Jesus Christ, or if all things are in him, that then those who possess Jesus Christ through faith, *have complete salvation in him.* Therefore, for any to assert, that Christ is not sufficient, but that something more is required besides him, would be too gross a blasphemy: for hence it would follow, that Christ was but half a Savior.

3. CANONS OF DORDT
   a. First Head of Doctrine, Article 7

Election is the unchangeable purpose of God, whereby, before the foundation of the world, he hath out of mere grace, according to the sovereign good pleasure of his own will, chosen, from the whole human race, which had fallen through their own fault, from their primitive state of rectitude, into sin and destruction, *a certain number of persons to redemption in Christ,* whom he from eternity appointed the Mediator and Head of the elect, and the foundation of salvation.

This elect number, though by nature neither better nor more deserving than others, but with them involved in one common misery, *God hath decreed to give to Christ, to be saved by him,* and effectually to call and draw them to his communion by his Word and Spirit, to bestow upon them true faith, justification and sanctification; and having powerfully preserved them in the fellowship of his Son, finally, to glorify them for the demonstration of his mercy, and for the praise of his glorious grace; as it is written: "According as he hath chosen us in him, before the foundation of the world, that we should be holy, and without blame before him in love; having predestinated us unto the adoption of children by Jesus Christ to himself, according to the good pleasure of his will, to the praise of the glory of his grace, wherein he hath made us accepted in the beloved" (Eph. 1:4–6). And elsewhere: "Whom he did predestinate, them he also called, and whom he called, them he also justified, and whom he justified, them he also glorified" (Rom. 8:30).

b. Second Head of Doctrine, Article 7

But as many as truly believe, and are delivered and saved from sin and destruction through the death of Christ, are indebted for this benefit solely to the grace of God, given them in Christ from everlasting, and not to any merit of their own.

c. Second Head of Doctrine, Article 8

For this was the sovereign counsel, and most gracious will and purpose of God the Father, that *the quickening and saving efficacy of the most precious death of his Son should extend to all the elect,* for bestowing *upon them alone* the gift of justifying faith, thereby to bring them infallibly to salvation: that is, it was the will of God, that Christ by the blood of the cross, whereby he confirmed the new covenant, should effectually redeem out of every people, tribe, nation, and language, *all those, and those only, who were from eternity chosen to salvation, and given to him by the Father;* that he should confer upon them faith, which together with all the other saving gifts of the Holy Spirit, he purchased for them by his death; should purge them from all sin, both original and actual, whether committed before or after believing; and having faithfully preserved them even to the end, should at last bring them free from every spot and blemish to the enjoyment of glory in his own presence forever.

d. Second Head of Doctrine, Rejection of Errors, Error 1

The true doctrine having been explained, the Synod rejects the errors of those who teach: That God the Father has ordained his Son to the death of the cross without a certain and definite decree to save any, so that the necessity, profitableness and worth of what Christ merited by his death might have existed, and might remain in all its parts complete, perfect and intact, even if the merited redemption had never in fact been applied to any person. For this doctrine tends to the despising of the wisdom of the Father and of the merits of Jesus Christ, and is contrary to Scripture. For thus saith our Savior: "I lay down my life for the sheep, and I know them" (John 10:15, 27). And the prophet Isaiah saith concerning the Savior: "When thou shalt make his soul an offering for sin, he shall see his seed, he shall prolong his days, and the pleasure of Jehovah shall prosper in his hand" (Isa. 53:10). Finally, this contradicts the article of faith according to which we believe the catholic Christian church.

e. Second Head of Doctrine, Rejection of Errors, Error 5
The true doctrine having been explained, the Synod rejects the errors of those who teach: That all men have been accepted unto the state of reconciliation and unto the grace of the covenant, so that no one is worthy of condemnation on account of original sin, and that no one shall be condemned because of it, but that all are free from the guilt of original sin. For this opinion is repugnant to Scripture, which teaches that we are by nature children of wrath (Eph. 2:3).

f. Second Head of Doctrine, Rejection of Errors, Error 6
The true doctrine having been explained, the Synod rejects the errors of those: Who use the difference between meriting and appropriating, to the end that they may instill into the minds of the imprudent and inexperienced this teaching that God, as far as he is concerned, has been minded of applying to all equally the benefits gained by the death of Christ; but that, while some obtain the pardon of sin and eternal life, and others do not, this difference depends on their own free will, which joins itself to the grace that is offered without exception, and that it is not dependent on the special gift of mercy, which powerfully works in them, that they rather than others should appropriate unto themselves this grace. For these, while they feign that they present this distinction, in a sound sense, seek to instill into the people the destructive poison of the Pelagian errors.

4. WESTMINSTER CONFESSION OF FAITH
a. Chapter 3, Article 6
As God hath appointed the elect unto glory, so hath he, by the eternal and most free purpose of his will, foreordained all the means thereunto. Wherefore they who are elected being fallen in Adam, are redeemed by Christ; are effectually called unto faith in Christ by his Spirit working in due season; are justified, adopted, sanctified, and kept by his power through

faith unto salvation. *Neither are any others redeemed by Christ, effectually called, justified, adopted, sanctified, and saved, but the elect only.*

(Scripture proofs: 1 Pet. 1:2; Eph. 1:4, 5; Eph. 2:10; 2 Thess. 2:13; 1 Thess. 5: 9, 10; Tit. 2:14; Rom. 8:30; Eph. 1:5; 2 Thess. 2:13; 1 Pet. 1:5; John 17:9; Rom. 8:28; John 6: 64, 65; John 10:26; John 8:47; 1 John 2:19.)

b. Chapter 8, Article 5

The Lord Jesus, by his perfect obedience and sacrifice of himself, which he through the eternal Spirit once offered up unto God, hath fully satisfied the justice of his Father; and purchased, not only reconciliation, but an everlasting inheritance in the kingdom of heaven, for *all those whom the Father hath given unto Him.*

(Scripture proofs: Rom. 5:19; Heb. 9:14, 16; Heb. 10:14; Eph. 5:2; Rom. 3:25, 26; Dan. 9:24, 26; Col. 1:19, 20; Eph. 1:11, 14; John 17:2; Heb. 9:12, 15.)

c. Chapter 8, Article 8

To all those for whom Christ hath purchased redemption, he doth certainly and effectually apply and communicate the same; making intercession for them; and revealing unto them, in and by the word, the mysteries of salvation; effectually persuading them by his Spirit to believe and obey; and governing their hearts by his word and Spirit; overcoming all their enemies by his almighty power and wisdom, in such manner and ways as are most consonant to his wonderful and unsearchable dispensation.

(Scripture proofs: John 6:37, 39; John 10:15, 16; 1 John 2:1, 2; Rom. 8:34; John 15:13, 15; Eph. 1:7–9; John 17:6; John 14:16; Heb. 12:2; 2 Cor. 4:13; Rom. 8:9, 14; Rom. 15:18, 19; John 17:17; Ps. 110:1; 1 Cor. 15:25, 26; Mal. 4:2, 3; Col. 2:15.)

d. Chapter 11, Article 3

Christ, by his obedience and death, did *fully discharge* the debt of *all those that are thus justified,* and did make a proper, real, and full satisfaction to his Father's justice in their behalf. Yet, in as much as he was given by the Father for them, and his obedience and satisfaction accepted in their stead, and both freely, not for any thing in them, their justification is only of free grace; that both the exact justice and rich grace of God might be glorified in the justification of sinners.

(Scripture proofs: Rom. 5:8–10, 19; 1 Tim. 2:5, 6; Heb. 10:10, 14; Dan. 9:24, 26; Isa. 53:4–6, 10–12; Rom. 8:32; 2 Cor. 5:21; Matt. 3:17; Eph. 5:2; Rom. 3:24; Eph. 1:7; Rom. 3:26; Eph. 2:7.)

e. Chapter 11, Article 4

God did, from all eternity, decree *to justify all the elect;* and Christ did, in the fulness of time, *die for their sins,* and rise again for their justification: nevertheless they are not justified, until the Holy Spirit doth in due time actually apply Christ unto them.

(Scripture proofs: Gal. 3:8; 1 Pet. 1:2, 19, 20; Rom. 8:30; Gal. 4:4; 1 Tim. 2:6; Rom. 4:25; Col. 1:21, 22; Gal. 2:16; Tit. 3:4–7.)

5. WESTMINSTER LARGER CATECHISM

a. *Question and Answer 38*

Q. Why was it requisite that the Mediator should be God?
A. It was requisite that the Mediator should be God, that he might sustain and keep the human nature from sinking under the infinite wrath of God, and the power of death; give worth and efficacy to his sufferings, obedience, and intercession; and to satisfy God's justice, procure his favour, *purchase a peculiar people,* give his Spirit to them, conquer all their enemies, and bring them to everlasting salvation.

(Scripture proofs: Acts 2:24, 25; Rom. 1:4; comp. with Rom. 4:25; Heb. 9:14; Acts 20:28; Heb. 9:14; Heb. 7:25–28; Rom. 3:24–26; Eph. 1:6; Matt. 3:17; Tit. 2:13, 14; Gal. 4:6; Luke 1:68, 69, 71, 74; Heb. 5:8, 9; Heb. 9:11–15.)

b. *Question and Answer 41*

Q. Why was our Mediator called Jesus?
A. Our Mediator was called Jesus, because he saveth *his people* from their sins.

(Scripture proof: Matt. 1:21.)

c. *Question and Answer 44*

Q. How doth Christ execute the office of a priest?
A. Christ executeth the office of a priest, in his once offering himself a sacrifice without spot to God, *to be a reconciliation* for the sins *of his people;* and in making continual intercession for them.

(Scripture proofs: Heb. 9:14, 28; Heb. 2:17; Heb. 7:25.)

d. *Question and Answer 46*
  Q. What was the estate of Christ's humiliation?
  A. The estate of Christ's humiliation was that low condition, wherein he *for our sakes,* emptying himself of his glory, took upon him the form of a servant, in his conception and birth, life, death, and after his death, until his resurrection.
  (Scripture proofs: Phil. 2:6–8; Luke 1:31; 2 Cor. 8:9; Acts 2:24.)

e. *Question and Answer 59*
  Q. Who are made partakers of redemption through Christ?
  A. Redemption is certainly applied, and effectually communicated, *to all those for whom Christ hath purchased it;* who are in time by the Holy Ghost enabled to believe in Christ according to the gospel.
  (Scripture proofs: Eph. 1:13, 14; John 6:37, 39; John 10:15, 16; Eph. 2:8; 2 Cor. 4:13.)

E. IRRESISTIBLE GRACE

1. HEIDELBERG CATECHISM

a. Lord's Day 1
  Question and Answer 1
  Q. What is thy only comfort in life and death?
  A. That I with body and soul, both in life and death, am not my own, but belong unto my faithful Savior Jesus Christ; who, with his precious blood, hath fully satisfied for all my sins, and delivered me from all the power of the devil; and so preserves me that without the will of my heavenly Father, not a hair can fall from my head; yea, that all things must be subservient to my salvation, and therefore, by his Holy Spirit, he also assures me of eternal life, and *makes me* sincerely willing and ready, henceforth, to live unto him.
  (Scripture proofs: 1 Cor. 6:19, 20; Rom. 14:7–9; 1 Cor. 3:23; 1 Pet. 1:18, 19; 1 John 1:7; 1 John 3:8; Heb. 2:14, 15; John 6:39; John 10:28, 29; Luke 21:18; Matt. 10:30; Rom. 8:28; 2 Cor. 1:22; 2 Cor. 5:5; Rom. 8:14; Rom. 7:22.)

b. Lord's Day 3
  Question and Answer 8
  Q. Are we then so corrupt that we are wholly incapable of doing any good, and inclined to all wickedness?

A. Indeed we are; except we are *regenerated by the Spirit of God.*

(Scripture proofs: Gen. 6:5; Job 14:4; Job 15:14, 16; John 3:5; Eph. 2:5.)

c. Lord's Day 20
Question and Answer 53
Q. What dost thou believe concerning the Holy Ghost?
A. First, that he is true and co-eternal God with the Father and the Son; secondly, that he is also given me, to *make me* by a true faith, partaker of Christ and all his benefits, that he may comfort me and abide with me for ever.

(Scripture proofs: Gen. 1:2; Isa. 48:16; 1 Cor. 3:16; Matt. 28:19; 2 Cor. 1:22; Gal. 3:14; 1 Pet. 1:2; Acts 9:31; John 14:16; 1 Pet. 4:14.)

d. Lord's Day 32
Question and Answer 86
Q. Since then we are delivered from our misery, *merely of grace,* through Christ, *without any merit of ours,* why must we still do good works?
A. Because Christ, having redeemed and delivered us by his blood, also renews us by his Holy Spirit, after his own image; that so we may testify, by the whole of our conduct, our gratitude to God for his blessings, and that he may be praised by us; also, that every one may be assured in himself of his faith, by the fruits thereof; and that, by our godly conversation, others may be gained to Christ.

(Scripture proofs: 1 Cor. 6:19, 20; Rom. 6:13; Rom. 12:1, 2; 1 Pet. 2:5, 9, 10; Matt. 5:16; 1 Pet. 2:12; 2 Pet. 1:10; Gal. 5:6, 24; 1 Pet. 3:1, 2; Matt. 5:16; Rom. 14:19.)

2. (BELGIC) CONFESSION OF FAITH
   a. Article 14
   . . . Therefore we reject all that is taught repugnant to this, concerning the free will of man, since man is but a slave to sin; and has nothing of himself, unless it is given from heaven. For who may presume to boast, that he of himself can do any good, since Christ saith, No man can come to me, except the Father, which hath sent me, draw him? Who will glory in his own will, who understands, that to be carnally minded is enmity against God? Who can speak of his knowledge, since

the natural man receiveth not the things of the spirit of God? In short, who dare suggest any thought, since he knows that we are not sufficient of ourselves to think anything as of ourselves, but that our sufficiency is of God? And therefore what the apostle saith ought justly to be held sure and firm, that God worketh in us both to will and to do of his good pleasure. *For there is no will nor understanding, conformable to the divine will and understanding, but what Christ hath wrought in man;* which he teaches us, when he saith, Without me ye can do nothing.

b. Article 22

We believe that, to attain the true knowledge of this great mystery, *the Holy Ghost kindleth in our hearts an upright faith,* which embraces Jesus Christ, with all his merits, appropriates him, and seeks nothing more besides him. For it must needs follow, either that all things, which are requisite to our salvation, are not in Jesus Christ, or if all things are in him, that then those who possess Jesus Christ through faith, have complete salvation in him. Therefore, for any to assert, that Christ is not sufficient, but that something more is required besides him, would be too gross a blasphemy: for hence it would follow, that Christ was but half a Savior.

c. Article 24

We believe that *this true faith being wrought in man by the hearing of the Word of God, and the operation of the Holy Ghost,* doth regenerate and make him a new man, causing him to live a new life, and freeing him from the bondage of sin. Therefore it is so far from being true, that this justifying faith makes men remiss in a pious and holy life, that on the contrary without it they would never do anything out of love to God, but only out of self-love or fear of damnation. Therefore it is impossible that this holy faith can be unfruitful in man: for we do not speak of a vain faith, but of such a faith, which is called in Scripture, a faith that worketh by love, which excites man to the practice of those works, which God has commanded in his Word. Which works, as they proceed from the good root of faith, are good and acceptable in the sight of God, forasmuch as they are all sanctified by his grace: howbeit they are of no account towards our justification. For it is by faith in Christ that we are justified, even before we do good works; otherwise they could not be good works, any more than the fruit of a tree can be good, before the tree itself is good. Therefore we do good works, but not to merit by them (for what can we merit?); nay, we are beholden to God for the good works we do, and not he to us, since it is he that worketh in us both to will and to do of his good pleasure. Let us therefore attend to what is written: when ye shall have done all those things which are commanded you, say, we are unprofitable servants; we have done that which was our duty to do. In the meantime, we do not deny that God rewards our good works, but it is through his grace that he crowns his gifts. Moreover, though we do good works, we do not found our salvation upon them; for we do no work but what is polluted by our flesh, and also punishable; and although we could perform such works, still the remembrance of one sin is sufficient to make God reject them. Thus then we would always be in doubt, tossed to and fro without any certainty, and our poor consciences continually vexed, if they relied not on the merits of the suffering and death of our Savior.

3. CANONS OF DORDT

The following three articles from the first chapter of the Canons show the relationship between irresistible grace and unconditional election, for an election that is truly unconditional demands a grace so powerful.

a. First Head of Doctrine, Article 6

That some receive the gift of faith from God, and others do not receive it proceeds from God's eternal decree, "For known unto God are all his works from the beginning of the world" (Acts 15:18). "Who worketh all things after the counsel of his own will" (Eph. 1:11). According to which decree, *he graciously softens the hearts of the elect, however obstinate, and inclines them to believe,* while he leaves the non-elect in his just judgment to their own wickedness and obduracy. And herein is especially displayed the profound, the merciful, and at the same time the righteous discrimination between men, equally involved in ruin; or that decree of election and reprobation, revealed in the Word of God, which though men of perverse, impure and unstable minds wrest to their own destruction, yet to holy and pious souls affords unspeakable consolation.

b. First Head of Doctrine, Article 7

Election is the unchangeable purpose of God, whereby, before the foundation of the world, he hath out of mere grace, according to the sovereign good pleasure of his own will, chosen, from the whole human race, which had fallen through their own fault, from their primitive state of rectitude, into sin and destruction, a certain number of persons to redemption in Christ, whom he from eternity appointed the Mediator and Head of the elect, and the foundation of salvation.

This elect number, though by nature neither better nor more deserving than others, but with them involved in one common misery, God hath decreed to give to Christ, to be saved by him, and *effectually to call and draw them to his communion by his Word and Spirit, to bestow upon them true faith, justification and sanctification;* and having powerfully preserved them in the fellowship of his Son, finally, to glorify them for the demonstration of his mercy, and for the praise of his glorious grace; as it is written: "According as he hath chosen us in him, before the foundation of the world, that we should be holy, and without blame before him in love; having predestinated us unto the adoption of children by Jesus Christ to himself, according to the good pleasure of his will, to the praise of the glory of his grace, wherein he hath made us accepted in the beloved" (Eph. 1:4–6). And elsewhere: "Whom he did predestinate, them he also called, and whom he called, them he also justified, and whom he justified, them he also glorified" (Rom. 8:30).

c. First Head of Doctrine, Article 8

There are not various decrees of election, but one and the same decree respecting all those, who shall be saved, both under the Old and New Testament: since the scripture declares the good pleasure, purpose and counsel of the divine will to be one, according to which he hath chosen us from eternity, *both to grace and glory, to salvation and the way of salvation, which he hath ordained that we should walk therein.*

Articles 7, 8, 9, and Rejection of Errors 6, all from the Second Head of Doctrine of the Canons, show how the atonement of Christ, limited to the elect, is made powerful and infallible by the irresistible grace of God.

d. Second Head of Doctrine, Article 7

But as many as truly believe, and are delivered and saved from sin and destruction through the death of Christ, are indebted for this benefit *solely to the grace of God,* given them in Christ from everlasting, and not to any merit of their own.

e. Second Head of Doctrine, Article 8

For this was the sovereign counsel, and most gracious will and purpose of God the Father, that the quickening and saving efficacy of the most precious death of his Son should extend to all the elect, for bestowing upon them alone the gift of justifying faith, thereby to bring them *infallibly* to salvation: that is, it was the will of God, that Christ by the blood of the cross, whereby he confirmed the new covenant, should *effectually redeem* out of every people, tribe, nation, and language, all those, and those only, who were from eternity chosen to salvation, and given to him by the Father; that he should *confer upon them faith,* which together with all the other saving gifts of the Holy Spirit, he purchased for them by his death; should purge them from all sin, both original and actual, whether committed before or after believing; and having faithfully preserved them even to the end, should at last bring them free from every spot and blemish to the enjoyment of glory in his own presence forever.

f. Second Head of Doctrine, Article 9

This purpose proceeding from everlasting love towards the elect, has from the beginning of the world to this day been *powerfully accomplished,* and will henceforward still continue to be accomplished, notwithstanding all the ineffectual opposition of the gates of hell, so that the elect in due time may be gathered together into one, and that there never may be wanting a church composed of believers, the foundation of which is laid in the blood of Christ, which may steadfastly love, and faithfully serve him as their Savior, who as a bridegroom for his bride, laid down his life for them upon the cross, and which may celebrate his praises here and through all eternity.

g. Second Head of Doctrine, Rejection of Errors, Error 6

The true doctrine having been explained, the Synod rejects the errors of those: Who use the difference between meriting and appropriating, to the end that they may instill into the minds of the imprudent and inexperienced this teaching that God, as far as he is concerned, has been minded of applying to all equally the benefits gained by the death of Christ; but that, while some obtain the pardon of sin and eternal life, and others do not, this difference depends on their own free will, which joins itself to the grace that is offered without exception, and that it is not dependent on the special gift of mercy, which powerfully works in them, that they rather than others should appropriate unto themselves this grace. For these, while they feign that they present this distinction, in a sound sense, seek to instill into the people the destructive poison of the Pelagian errors.

h. Third and Fourth Heads of Doctrine, Article 10

But that others who are called by the gospel, obey the call, and are converted, is not to be ascribed to the proper exercise of free will, whereby one distinguishes himself above others, equally furnished with grace sufficient for faith and conversions, as the proud heresy of Pelagius maintains; but *it must be wholly ascribed to God,* who as he has chosen his own from eternity in Christ, so he *confers* upon them faith and repentance, rescues them from the power of darkness, and translates them into the kingdom of his own Son, that they may show forth the praises of him, who hath called them out of darkness into his marvelous light; and may glory not in themselves, but in the Lord according to the testimony of the apostles in various places.

i. Third and Fourth Heads of Doctrine, Article 11
    But when God accomplishes his good pleasure in the elect, or works in them true conversion, he not only causes the gospel to be externally preached to them, and *powerfully* illuminates their minds by his Holy Spirit, that they may rightly understand and discern the things of the Spirit of God; but by the *efficacy* of the same regenerating Spirit, pervades the inmost recesses of the man; he opens the closed, and softens the hardened heart, and circumcises that which was uncircumcised, infuses new qualities into the will, which though heretofore dead, he quickens; from being evil, disobedient, and refractory, he renders it good, obedient, and pliable; actuates and strengthens it, that like a good tree, it may bring forth the fruits of good actions.

j. Third and Fourth Heads of Doctrine, Article 12
    And this is the regeneration so highly celebrated in Scripture, and denominated a new creation: a resurrection from the dead, a making alive, which God works in us without our aid. But this is in no wise effected merely by the external preaching of the gospel, by moral suasion, or such a mode of operation, that after God has performed his part, it still remains in the power of man to be regenerated or not, to be converted, or to continue unconverted; but it is evidently a supernatural work, *most powerful,* and at the same time most delightful, astonishing, mysterious, and ineffable; not inferior in efficacy to creation, or the resurrection from the dead, as the Scripture inspired by the author of this work declares; so that *all in whose heart God works in this marvelous manner, are certainly, infallibly, and effectually regenerated, and do actually believe.* Whereupon the will thus renewed, is not only actuated and influenced by God, but in consequence of this influence, becomes itself active. Wherefore also, man is himself rightly said to believe and repent, by virtue of that grace received.

k. Third and Fourth Heads of Doctrine, Article 13

The manner of this operation cannot be fully comprehended by believers in this life. Notwithstanding which, they rest satisfied with knowing and experiencing, that by this grace of God they are *enabled* to believe with the heart, and love their Savior.

l. Third and Fourth Heads of Doctrine, Article 14

Faith is therefore to be considered as the gift of God, not on account of its being offered by God to man, to be accepted or rejected at his pleasure; but because it is in reality conferred, breathed, and infused into him; or even because God bestows the power or ability to believe, and then expects that man should by the exercise of his own free will, consent to the terms of salvation, and actually believe in Christ; but because he who works in man both to will and to do, and indeed all things in all, produces both the will to believe, and the act of believing also.

m. Third and Fourth Heads of Doctrine, Article 16

But as man by the fall did not cease to be a creature, endowed with understanding and will, nor did sin which pervaded the whole race of mankind, deprive him of the human nature, but brought upon him depravity and spiritual death; so also this grace of regeneration does not treat men as senseless stocks and blocks, nor takes away their will and its properties, neither does violence thereto; but *spiritually quickens, heals, corrects, and at the same time sweetly and powerfully bends* it; that where carnal rebellion and resistance formerly prevailed, a ready and sincere spiritual obedience begins to reign; in which the true and spiritual restoration and freedom of our will consist. Wherefore unless the admirable author of every good work wrought in us, man could have no hope of recovering from his fall by his own free will, by the abuse of which, in a state of innocence, he plunged himself into ruin.

n. Third and Fourth Heads of Doctrine, Article 17

As the almighty operation of God, whereby he prolongs and supports this our natural life, does not exclude, but requires the use of means, by which God of his infinite mercy and goodness hath chosen to exert his influence, so also the beforementioned supernatural operation of God, by which we are regenerated, in no wise excludes, or subverts the use of the gospel, which the most wise God has ordained to be the seed of regeneration, and food of the soul. Wherefore, as the apostles, and teachers who succeeded them, piously instructed the people concerning this grace of God, to his glory, and the abasement of all pride, and in the meantime, however, neglected not to keep them by the sacred precepts of the gospel in the exercise of the Word, sacraments and discipline; so even to this day, be it far from either instructors or instructed to presume to tempt God in the church by separating what he of his good pleasure hath most intimately joined together. For grace is conferred by means of admonitions; and the more readily we perform our duty, the more eminent usually is this blessing of God working in us, and the more directly is his work advanced; to whom alone all the glory both of means, and of their saving fruit and efficacy is forever due. Amen.

o. Third and Fourth Heads of Doctrine, Rejection of Errors, Error 6

The true doctrine having been explained, the Synod rejects the errors of those who teach: That in the true conversion of man no new qualities, powers or gifts can be infused by God into the will, and that therefore faith through which we are first converted, and because of which we are called believers, is not a quality or gift infused by God, but only an act of man, and that it can not be said to be a gift, except in respect of the power to attain to this faith. For thereby they contradict the Holy Scriptures, which declare that God infuses new qualities of faith, of obedience, and of the consciousness of his love into our hearts: "I will put my law in their inward parts, and in their hearts will I write it" (Jer. 31:33). And: "I will pour water upon him that is thirsty, and streams upon the dry ground; I will pour my Spirit upon thy seed" (Isa. 44:3). And: "The love of God hath been shed abroad in our hearts through the Holy Spirit which hath been given us" (Rom.

5:5). This is also repugnant to the continuous practice of the Church, which prays by the mouth of the Prophet thus: "Turn thou me, and I shall be turned" (Jer. 31:18).

p. Third and Fourth Heads of Doctrine, Rejection of Errors, Error 7

The true doctrine having been explained, the Synod rejects the errors of those who teach: That the grace whereby we are converted to God is only a gentle advising, or (as others explain it), that this is the noblest manner of working in the conversion of man, and that this manner of working, which consists in advising, is most in harmony with man's nature; and that there is no reason why this advising grace alone should not be sufficient to make the natural man spiritual, indeed, that God does not produce the consent of the will except through this manner of advising; and that the power of the divine working, whereby it surpasses the working of Satan, consists in this, that God promises eternal, while Satan promises only temporal goods. But this is altogether Pelagian and contrary to the whole Scripture which, besides this, teaches yet another and far more powerful and divine manner of the Holy Spirit's working in the conversion of man, as in Ezekiel: "A new heart also will I give you, and a new spirit will I put within you; and I will take away the stony heart out of your flesh, and I will give you a heart of flesh" (Ezek. 36:26).

q. Third and Fourth Heads of Doctrine, Rejection of Errors, Error 8

The true doctrine having been explained, the Synod rejects the errors of those who teach: That God in the regeneration of man does not use such powers of his omnipotence as potently and infallibly bend man's will to faith and conversion; but that all the works of grace having been accomplished, which God employs to convert man, man may yet so resist God and the Holy Spirit, when God intends man's regeneration and wills to regenerate him, and indeed that man often does so resist that he prevents entirely his regeneration, and that it therefore remains in man's power to be regenerated or not. For this is nothing less than the denial of all the efficiency of God's grace in our conversion, and the subjecting of the working of the Almighty God to the will of man, which is contrary to the Apostles, who teach: "That we believe according to the working of the strength of his power" (Eph. 1:19). And: "That God fulfills every desire of goodness and every work of faith with power" (2 Thess. 1:11). And: "That his divine power hath given unto us all things that pertain unto life and godliness" (2 Pet. 1:3).

r. Third and Fourth Heads of Doctrine, Rejection of Errors, Error 9

The true doctrine having been explained, the Synod rejects the errors of those who teach: That grace and free will are partial causes, which together work the beginning of conversion, and that grace, in order of working, does not precede the working of the will; that is, that God does not efficiently help the will of man unto conversion until the will of man moves and determines to do this. For the ancient Church has long ago condemned this doctrine of the Pelagians according to the words of the Apostle: "So then it is not of him that willeth, nor of him that runneth, but of God that hath mercy" (Rom. 9:16). Likewise: "For who maketh thee to differ? and what hast thou that thou didst not receive?" (1 Cor. 4:7). And: "For it is God who worketh in you both to will and to work, for his good pleasure" (Phil. 2:13).

4. WESTMINSTER CONFESSION OF FAITH

a. Chapter 3, Article 6

As God hath appointed the elect unto glory, so hath he, by the eternal and most free purpose of his will, foreordained all the means thereunto. Wherefore they who are elected being fallen in Adam, are redeemed by Christ; are *effectually* called unto faith in Christ by his Spirit working in due season; are justified, adopted, sanctified, and kept *by his power* through faith unto salvation. Neither are any others redeemed by Christ, effectually called, justified, adopted, sanctified and saved, but the elect only.

(Scripture proofs: 1 Pet. 1:2; Eph. 1:4, 5; Eph. 2:10; 2 Thess. 2:13; 1 Thess. 5:9, 10; Tit. 2:14; Rom. 8:30; Eph. 1:5; 2 Thess. 2:13; 1 Pet. 1:5; John 17:9; Rom. 8:28; John 6:64, 65; John 10:26; John 8:47; 1 John 2:19.)

b. Chapter 8, Article 8

To all those for whom Christ hath purchased redemption, *he doth certainly and effectually apply and communicate the same;* making intercession for them; and revealing unto them, in and by the word, the mysteries of salvation; *effectually* persuading them by his Spirit to believe and obey; and governing their hearts by His word and Spirit; overcoming all their enemies by his almighty power and wisdom, in such manner and ways as are most consonant to his wonderful and unsearchable dispensation.

(Scripture proofs: John 6:37, 39; John 10:15, 16; 1 John 2:1, 2; Rom. 8:34; John 15:13, 15; Eph. 1:7–9; John 17:6; John 14:16; Heb. 12:2; 2 Cor. 4:13; Rom. 8:9, 14; Rom. 15:18, 19; John 17:17; Ps. 110:1; 1 Cor. 15:25, 26; Mal. 4:2, 3; Col. 2:15.)

c. Chapter 9, Article 3

Man, by his fall into a state of sin, hath wholly lost all ability of will to any spiritual good accompanying salvation: so as a natural man, being altogether averse from that good, and dead in sin, is not able, by his own strength, to convert himself, or to prepare himself thereunto.

(Scripture proofs: Rom. 5:6; Rom. 8:7; John 15:5; Rom. 3:10, 12; Eph. 2:1, 5; Col. 2:13; John 6:44, 65; Eph. 2:2–5; 1 Cor. 2:14; Tit. 3:3–5.)

d. Chapter 9, Article 4

When God converts a sinner, and translates him into the state of grace, He freeth him from his natural bondage under sin, and *by his grace alone* enables him freely to will and to do that which is spiritually good; yet so as that, by reason of his remaining corruption, he doth not perfectly nor only will that which is good, but doth also will that which is evil.

(Scripture proofs: Col. 1:13; John 8:34, 36; Phil. 2:13; Rom. 6:18, 22; Gal. 5:17; Rom. 7:15, 18, 19, 21, 23.)

e. Chapter 9, Article 5

The will of man is made perfectly and immutably free to do good alone in the state of glory only.

(Scripture proofs: Eph. 4:13; Heb. 12:23; 1 John 3:2; Jude 24.)

5. WESTMINSTER LARGER CATECHISM
   a. *Question and Answer 59*
   Q. Who are made partakers of redemption through Christ?
   A. Redemption is *certainly applied, and effectually commu-nicated,* to all those for whom Christ hath purchased it; who are in *time by the Holy Ghost enabled to believe in Christ* according to the gospel.

   (Scripture proofs: Eph. 1:13, 14; John 6:37, 39; John 10:15, 16; Eph. 2:8; 2 Cor. 4:13.)

F. THE PERSEVERANCE OF THE SAINTS

1. HEIDELBERG CATECHISM
   a. Lord's Day 1
   Question and Answer 1
   Q. What is thy only comfort in life and death?
   A. That I with body and soul, both in life and death, am not my own, but belong unto my faithful Savior Jesus Christ; who, with his precious blood, hath fully satisfied for all my sins, and delivered me from all the power of the devil; and so *preserves me* that without the will of my heavenly Father, not a hair can fall from my head; yea, that all things must be subservient to my salvation, and therefore, by his Holy Spirit, he also *assures me of eternal life,* and makes me sincerely willing and ready, henceforth, to live unto him.

   (Scripture proofs: 1 Cor. 6:19, 20; Rom. 14:7–9; 1 Cor. 3:23; 1 Pet. 1:18, 19; 1 John 1:7; 1 John 3:8; Heb. 2:14, 15; John 6:39; John 10:28, 29; Luke 21:18; Matt. 10:30; Rom. 8:28; 2 Cor. 1:22; 2 Cor. 5:5; Rom. 8:14; Rom. 7:22.)

   b. Lord's Day 12
   Question and Answer 31
   Q. Why is he called Christ, that is anointed?
   A. Because he is ordained of God the Father, and anointed with the Holy Ghost, to be our chief Prophet and Teacher, who has fully revealed to us the secret counsel and will of God concerning our redemption; and to be our only High Priest, who by the one sacrifice of his body, has redeemed us, and makes continual intercession with the Father for us; and also to be our eternal King, who governs us by his word and Spirit, and who defends and *preserves* us in (the enjoyment of) that salvation, he has purchased for us.

(Scripture proofs: Heb. 1:9; Deut. 18:18; Acts 3:22; John 1:18; John 15:15; Matt. 11:27; Ps. 110:4; Heb. 7:21; Heb. 10:14; Rom. 8:34; Ps. 2:6; Luke 1:33; Matt. 28:18; John 10:28.)

c. Lord's Day 18
   Question and Answer 49
   Q. Of what advantage to us is Christ's ascension into heaven?
   A. First, that he is our advocate in the presence of his Father in heaven; secondly, that we have our flesh in heaven as a *sure pledge* that he, as the head, will also take up to himself, us, his members; thirdly, that he sends us his Spirit as an earnest, by whose power we "seek the things which are above, where Christ sitteth on the right hand of God, and not things on earth."
   (Scripture proofs: Heb. 9:24; 1 John 2:2; Rom. 8:34; John 14:2; Eph. 2:6; John 14:16; 2 Cor. 1:22; 2 Cor. 5:5; Col. 3:1; Phil. 3:20.)

d. Lord's Day 19
   Question and Answer 51
   Q. What profit is this glory of Christ [his exaltation], our head, unto us?
   A. First, that by his Holy Spirit he pours out heavenly graces upon us his members; and then that by his power he *defends and preserves us* against all enemies.
   (Scripture proofs: Eph. 4:8; Ps. 2:9; John 10:28.)

e. Lord's Day 21
   Question and Answer 54
   Q. What believest thou concerning the "holy catholic church" of Christ?
   A. That the Son of God from the beginning to the end of the world, gathers, defends, and *preserves* to himself by his Spirit and word, out of the whole human race, a church chosen to *everlasting life,* agreeing in true faith; and that I am and *for ever shall remain,* a living member thereof.
   (Scripture proofs: John 10:11; Gen. 26:4; Rom. 9:24; Eph. 1:10; John 10:16; Isa. 59:21; Deut. 10:14, 15; Acts 13:48; 1 Cor. 1:8, 9; Rom. 8:35ff.)

f. Lord's Day 22
Question and Answer 58
Q. What comfort takest thou from the article of "life ever-lasting"?
A. That since I now feel in my heart the beginning of eternal joy, after this life, *I shall inherit perfect salvation,* which "eye hath not seen, nor ear heard, neither hath it entered into the heart of man" to conceive, and that, to praise God therein for ever.
(Scripture proofs: 2 Cor. 5:2, 3, 6; Rom. 14:17; Ps. 10:11; 1 Cor. 2:9.)

g. Lord's Day 52
Question and Answer 127
Q. Which is the sixth petition [of the Lord's Prayer]?
A. "And lead us not into temptation, but deliver us from evil"; that is, since we are so weak in ourselves, that we cannot stand a moment; and besides this, since our mortal enemies, the devil, the world, and our own flesh, cease not to assault us, do thou *therefore preserve* and strengthen us by the power of thy Holy Spirit, that we may not be overcome in this spiritual warfare, but constantly and strenuously may resist our foes, till at last we obtain a complete victory.
(Scripture proofs: Matt. 6:13; Rom. 8:26; Ps. 103:14; 1 Pet. 5:8; Eph. 6:12; John 15:19; Rom. 7:23; Gal. 5:17; Matt. 26:41; Mark 13:33; 1 Thess. 3:13; 1 Thess. 5:23.)

2. (BELGIC) CONFESSION OF FAITH
a. Article 27
We believe and profess, one catholic or universal Church, which is an holy congregation, of true Christian believers, all expecting their salvation in Jesus Christ, being washed by his blood, sanctified and *sealed* by the Holy Ghost. This Church hath been from the beginning of the world, and will be to the end thereof; which is evident from this, that Christ is an eternal King, which, without subjects, cannot be. And this holy Church is *preserved* or supported by God, against the rage of the whole world; though she sometimes (for a while) appears very small, and in the eyes of men, to be reduced to nothing: as during the perilous reign of Ahab, the Lord reserved unto him seven thousand men, who had not bowed their knees to

Baal. Furthermore, this holy Church is not confined, bound, or limited to a certain place or to certain persons, but is spread and dispersed over the whole world; and yet is joined and united with heart and will, by the power of faith, in one and the same spirit.

3. CANONS OF DORDT
   a. First Head of Doctrine, Article 7
      ... This elect number, though by nature neither better nor more deserving than others, but with them involved in one common misery, God hath decreed to give to Christ, to be saved by him, and effectually to call and draw them to his communion by his Word and Spirit, to bestow upon them true faith, justification and sanctification; and having *powerfully preserved* them in the fellowship of his Son, finally, to glorify them for the demonstration of his mercy, and for the praise of his glorious grace; as it is written: "According as he hath chosen us in him, before the foundation of the world, that we should be holy, and without blame before him in love; having predestinated us unto the adoption of children by Jesus Christ to himself, according to the good pleasure of his will, to the praise of the glory of his grace, wherein he hath made us accepted in the beloved" (Eph. 1:4–6). And elsewhere: "Whom he did predestinate, them he also called, and whom he called, them he also justified, and whom he justified, them he also glorified" (Rom. 8:30).

   b. First Head of Doctrine, Article 11
      And as God himself is most wise, unchangeable, omniscient and omnipotent, so the election made by him can neither be interrupted nor changed, recalled or annulled; *neither can the elect be cast away, nor their number diminished.*

   c. First Head of Doctrine, Rejection of Errors, Error 6
      The true doctrine concerning Election and Rejection having been explained, the Synod rejects the errors of those who teach: That not every election unto salvation is unchangeable, but that some of the elect, any decree of God notwithstanding, can yet perish and do indeed perish. By which gross er-

ror they make God to be changeable, and destroy the comfort which the godly obtain out of the firmness of their election, and contradict the Holy Scripture, which teaches, that the elect can not be led astray (Matt. 24:24); that Christ does not lose those whom the Father gave him (John 6:39); and that God hath also glorified those whom he foreordained, called and justified (Rom. 8:30).

These articles from the Canons are especially valuable because they demonstrate the connection between unconditional election and the perseverance of saints, just as the next article shows the connection between perseverance and limited atonement.

d. Second Head of Doctrine, Article 8
For this was the sovereign counsel, and most gracious will and purpose of God the Father, that the quickening and saving efficacy of the most precious death of his Son should extend to all the elect, for bestowing upon them alone the gift of justifying faith, thereby to bring them infallibly to salvation: that is, it was the will of God, that Christ by the blood of the cross, whereby he confirmed the new covenant, should effectually redeem out of every people, tribe, nation, and language, all those, and those only, who were from eternity chosen to salvation, and given to him by the Father; that he should confer upon them faith, which together with all the other saving gifts of the Holy Spirit, he purchased for them by his death; should purge them from all sin, both original and actual, whether committed before or after believing; and having *faithfully preserved them even to the end,* should at last bring them free from every spot and blemish to the enjoyment of glory in his own presence forever.

The remaining articles are from the Fifth Head of Doctrine, the chapter on the perseverance of the saints.

e. Fifth Head of Doctrine, Article 3
By reason of these remains of indwelling sin, and the temptations of sin and of the world, those who are converted could not persevere in a state of grace, if left to their own strength.

But God is faithful, who having conferred grace, *mercifully confirms,* and *powerfully preserves* them therein, even to the end.

f. Fifth Head of Doctrine, Article 6

But God, who is rich in mercy, according to his unchangeable purpose of election, does not wholly withdraw the Holy Spirit from his own people, even in their melancholy falls; nor suffers them to proceed so far as to lose the grace of adoption, and forfeit the state of justification, or to commit the sin unto death; nor does he permit them to be totally deserted, and to plunge themselves into everlasting destruction.

g. Fifth Head of Doctrine, Article 7

For in the first place, in these falls he preserves in them the incorruptible seed of regeneration from perishing, or being totally lost; and again, by his Word and Spirit, certainly and effectually renews them to repentance, to a sincere and godly sorrow for their sins, that they may seek and obtain remission in the blood of the Mediator, may again experience the favor of a reconciled God, through faith adore his mercies, and henceforward more diligently work out their own salvation with fear and trembling.

h. Fifth Head of Doctrine, Article 8

Thus, it is not in consequence of their own merits, or strength, but of God's free mercy, that they do not totally fall from faith and grace, nor continue and perish finally in their backslidings; which, with respect to themselves, is not only possible, but would undoubtedly happen; but with respect to God, it is utterly impossible, since his counsel cannot be changed, nor his promise fail, neither can the call according to his purpose be revoked, nor the merit, intercession and preservation of Christ be rendered ineffectual, nor the sealing of the Holy Spirit be frustrated or obliterated.

i. Fifth Head of Doctrine, Rejection of Errors, Error 3

The true doctrine having been explained, the Synod rejects the errors of those who teach: That the true believers

and regenerate not only can fall from justifying faith and
likewise from grace and salvation wholly and to the end, but
indeed often do fall from this and are lost forever. For this
conception makes powerless the grace, justification, regeneration, and continued keeping by Christ, contrary to the expressed words of the Apostle Paul: "That while we were yet
sinners Christ died for us. Much more then, being justified
by his blood, shall we be saved from the wrath of God
through him" (Rom. 5:8, 9). And contrary to the Apostle
John: "Whosoever is begotten of God doeth no sin, because
his seed abideth in him; and he can not sin, because he is begotten of God" (1 John 3:9). And also contrary to the words
of Jesus Christ: "I give unto them eternal life; and they shall
never perish, and no one shall snatch them out of my hand.
My Father who hath given them to me, is greater than all;
and no one is able to snatch them out of the Father's hand"
(John 10:28, 29).

4. WESTMINSTER CONFESSION OF FAITH
a. Chapter 17, Article 1

They whom God hath accepted in his Beloved, effectually
called and sanctified by his Spirit, *can neither totally nor finally fall away from the state of grace; but shall certainly persevere therein to the end, and be eternally saved.*

(Scripture proofs: Phil. 1:6; 2 Pet. 1:10; John 10:28, 29; 1 John 3:9; 1 Pet. 1:5,
9.)

b. Chapter 17, Article 2

This *perseverance of the saints* depends not upon their
own free will, but upon the immutability of the decree of election, flowing from the free and unchangeable love of God the
Father; upon the efficacy of the merit and intercession of Jesus Christ; the abiding of the Spirit, and of the seed of God
within them; and the nature of the covenant of grace: from
all which ariseth also the certainty and infallibility thereof.

(Scripture proofs: 2 Tim. 2:18, 19; Jer. 31:3; Heb. 10:10, 14; Heb. 13:20, 21;
Heb. 9:12, 13–15; Rom. 8:33–39; John 17:11, 24; Luke 22:32; Heb. 7:25;
John 14:16, 17; 1 John 2:27; 1 John 3:9; Jer. 32:40; John 10:28; 2 Thess. 3:3;
1 John 2:19.)

5. WESTMINSTER LARGER CATECHISM
   a. *Question and Answer 79*

   Q. May not true believers, by reason of their imperfections, and the many temptations and sins they are overtaken with, fall away from a state of grace?

   A. True believers, by reason of the unchangeable love of God, and His decree and covenant to give them *perseverance,* their inseparable union with Christ, his continual intercession for them, and the Spirit and seed of God abiding in them, *can neither totally nor finally fall away from the state of grace, but are kept by the power of God through faith unto salvation.*

   (Scripture proofs: Jer. 31:3; 2 Tim. 2:19; Heb. 13:20, 21; 2 Sam. 23:5; 1 Cor. 1:8, 9; Heb. 7:25; Luke 22:32; 1 John 3:9; 1 John 2:27; Jer. 32:40; John 10:28; 1 Pet. 1:5.)

   b. *Question and Answer 80*

   Q. Can true believers be infallibly assured that they are in the estate of grace, and that they *shall persevere* therein unto salvation?

   A. Such as truly believe in Christ, and endeavour to walk in all good conscience before him, may, without extraordinary revelation, by faith grounded upon the truth of God's promises, and by the Spirit enabling them to discern in themselves those graces to which the promises of life are made, and bearing witness with their spirits that they are the children of God, be *infallibly assured that they are in the estate of grace, and shall persevere therein unto salvation.*

   (Scripture proofs: 1 John 2:3; 1 Cor. 2:12; 1 John 3:14, 18, 19, 21, 24; 1 John 4:13, 16; Heb. 6:11, 12; Rom. 8:16; 1 John 5:13.)

Index of Citations
from the Creeds

Index of Scripture References
in Chapters 1–6

Saved by Grace